Settlement Types in Post-Roman Scotland

Lloyd R. Laing

British Archaeological Reports 13
1975

British Archaeological Reports

122 Banbury Road, Oxford OX2 7BP, England

GENERAL EDITORS

A.C.C. Brodribb, M.A.   A.R. Hands, B.Sc., M.A., D.Phil.
Mrs. Y.M. Hands   D.R. Walker, B.A.

ADVISORY EDITORS

C.B. Burgess, M.A.   Neil Cossons, M.A., F.S.A., F.M.A.
Professor B.W. Cunliffe, M.A., Ph.D., F.S.A.
Sonia Chadwick Hawkes, B.A., M.A., F.S.A.
Professor G.D.B. Jones, M.A., D.Phil., F.S.A.
Frances Lynch, M.A., F.S.A.   P.A. Mellars, M.A., Ph.D.
P.A. Rahtz, M.A., F.S.A.

B.A.R. 13, 1975: "Settlement Types in Post-Roman Scotland."

© Lloyd R. Laing, 1975.

ISBN 9780904531138 paperback
ISBN 9781407317526 e-book
DOI https://doi.org/10.30861/9780904531138
A catalogue record for this book is available from the British Library
This book is available at www.barpublishing.com

SETTLEMENT TYPES IN POST-ROMAN SCOTLAND

CONTENTS

LIST OF FIGURES

SUMMARY

It is suggested that there is archaeological evidence for the continuity of Iron Age settlement types in Scotland into the post-Roman period, and that although certain intrusive settlement types can be recognised, notably the Norse house and the Early Christian timber hall, these were the products of intrusive social groups and had little lasting impact on the settlement pattern of post-Roman Scotland as a whole. It is suggested that this evidence from settlements can be equated with the evidence of material assemblages and the historical evidence for the growth of the post-Roman kingdoms to build up a cumulative picture of cultural continuity throughout the first millennium A.D. , a situation matched in Ireland by the persistence of the economy and settlement pattern represented by raths. Although certain types of Iron Age settlement persist into the later medieval and post-medieval period in Scotland, the evidence suggests that the occupation of Iron Age sites was of quite a different character from the original occupation and as such can only be taken as evidence for continuity of population distribution and not of the Iron Age social and economic structure, at least in the areas dominated by the Scotto-Norman kings.

SETTLEMENTS AND FORTS OF THE EARLY
CHRISTIAN PERIOD

In the last ten years excavations on sites in south-west England have stimulated discussion on the subject of the re-occupation of hillforts in the post-Roman period, the results of which are now conveniently summarized in print (Fowler, 1971; Rahtz & Fowler, 1972; Alcock, 1971, 209-229; Alcock, 1972, 174-93). The post-Roman re-occupation of Welsh hillforts has long been known, and is clearly demonstrated at Dinas Powys (Alcock, 1963), Dinas Emrys (Savory, 1960) and less clearly at Dinorben (Gardner & Savory, 1964), Coygan Camp (Wainwright, 1967) and at Degannwy (Alcock, 1967). This phenomenon has been set in its historical context in a number of studies, notably by Alcock (Alcock, 1965; Alcock, 1970). In Scotland, while it has been admitted that some fortified sites were undoubtedly re-occupied (if not occupied for the first time) in the post-Roman period, there has been considerable debate over what categories of sites were occupied in the post-Roman period, and the nature of their defences. In the light of recent excavations, it is perhaps not premature to consider some of these controversies anew.

NUCLEAR FORTS

In a now classic study R.B.K. Stevenson drew attention to the similarities in the character of the defences on a group of Scottish sites which he called 'nuclear forts' (Stevenson, 1948-9). The essence of a nuclear fort lies in its having usually a central citadel linked to a series of outer enclosures constructed with stretches of walling which make use of the natural defences of the rock on which they are sited. Some of the enclosures may be angular, and the walls can show differing construction techniques according to the needs of the terrain, but characteristic are walls backed onto hillsides with the earth terraced out level behind them and walls 'so fitted above natural rock faces that we might overlook them unless we note that their length lies horizontally whereas the longest natural lines and cracks are vertical' (Stevenson, 1948-9, 191). Stevenson discussed four main sites: Dalmahoy (Midlothian), Dunadd (Argyll), Dundurn (Perthshire) (Figs. 1-3) and Ruberslaw (Roxburghshire), and pointed out that there was historical evidence for the occupation of Dunadd and Dundurn in the Early Christian period, archaeological evidence from the former, and a limited amount of archaeological evidence from Dalmahoy in the form of a gold stud cap and a fragment of a mould of clay from the citadel (Stevenson, op.cit., 195-8). This brief list was extended in 1955 by R. Feachem in his survey of the fortifications of Pictland (Feachem, 1955), where he discussed in addition

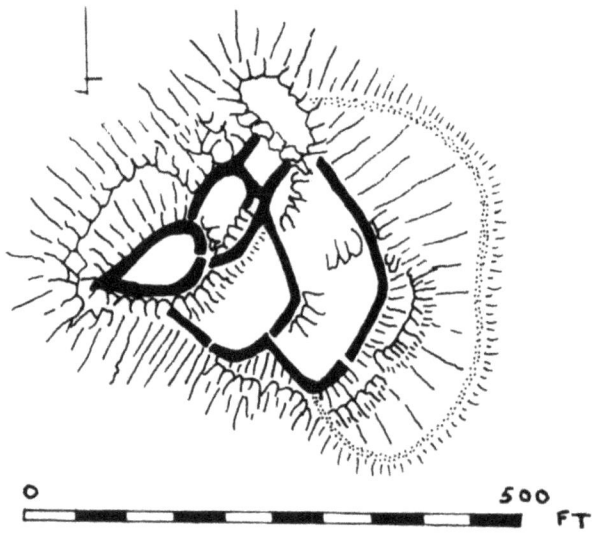

0   500
FT

Fig. 1.   Dunadd

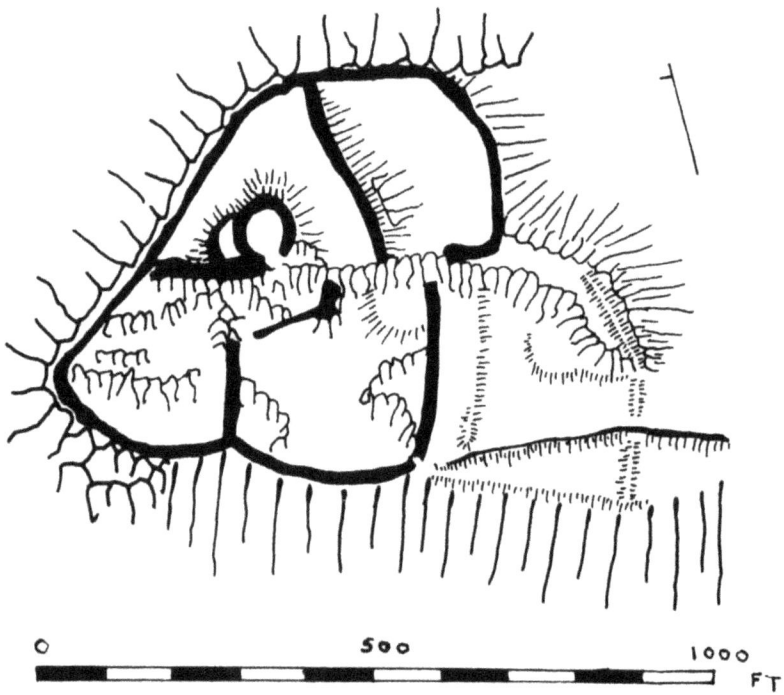

0   500   1000
FT

Fig. 2.   Dundurn

to the two main nuclear forts of Dunadd and Dundurn a series of structures which he described as 'ring forts' - stone walled forts set within walls or ramparts enclosing larger areas. These he discussed at much greater length in 1967, when he declared that 'Dunadd and Dundurn represent early Iron Age hillforts the defences of which may have been repaired or improved' (Feachem, 1967, 85). He suggested that all 'citadel' sites belong to the Roman Iron Age (Feachem, 1967, 84). In his discussion of Dunadd and Dundurn he suggested that Dunadd could not have been built initially in the post-Roman period because (a) there were Roman finds from the site, (b) there was no evidence that hillforts were still being constructed in the post-Roman period and (c) there were no forts like it in Ulster, from whence the Dalriadic Scots who occupied Dunadd in the post-Roman period came.

These three objections no longer remain valid. (1) The 'Roman material' from Dunadd consists of four small fragments of samian pottery (Craw, 1929-30, 124). Samian was apparently re-used in the Early Christian period as a colouring material, and thus need not represent the last phase of the Iron Age. There is samian from the Mote of Mark, Kirkcudbright (Curle, 1913-14, 161), the defences of which recent excavation have shown to be of the post-Roman period (Laing, 1973), from the undoubtedly Early Christian period crannogs at Lagore (Hencken, 1950, 123) and Lough Faughan (Collins, 1955, 55), at Dinas Powys (Alcock, 1963, 22) and more recently at Cadbury Congresbury, Somerset (Fowler, 1970, 342) and Kiondroghad, Isle of Man (Gelling, 1969, 81). Samian is also ubiquitous on Anglo-Saxon sites (for a list of examples, see Alcock, 1963, 22). (2) The second point is clearly disproved by a series of sites in Scotland which have undoubted post-Roman occupation and, in a few cases, post-Roman construction. (3) The third point is to some extent irrelevant; the Irish settlers in Western Scotland need not necessarily have constructed fortifications modelled on native Ulster prototypes. Not enough work has been yet done on Irish hillforts (see Raftery, 1972, for preliminary review), but some evidence for the post-Roman occupation of forts in Ulster is now available, notably from Downpatrick (Proudfoot, 1956).

If Feachem's objections to Dunadd being of post-Roman construction are invalid, are there any alternative objections that can be raised? The earliest find from the site is a carved stone ball of a type generally held to be secondary neolithic on the somewhat tenuous evidence of similar finds from Skara Brae. Such objects have been plotted and discussed by Atkinson (Atkinson, 1962, 28 and Fig. 5), and the attribution is probably not in doubt, though the distribution is remarkably similar to that of the Pictish symbol stones and a post-Roman date for at least some may remain a possibility. In addition there is a single sherd of a Food Vessel (Craw, 1929-30, 123). Neither of these finds can be related to an occupation phase, and the remainder would all be in keeping with an occupation from the fifth to the ninth centuries A.D.

A few of the finds are possibly of types current in both the Iron Age and the Early Christian period; of these the projecting ring-headed pin (Christison, 1904-5, Fig. 49) is the most outstanding. Projecting ring-headed pins appear to have been produced first in the second or first

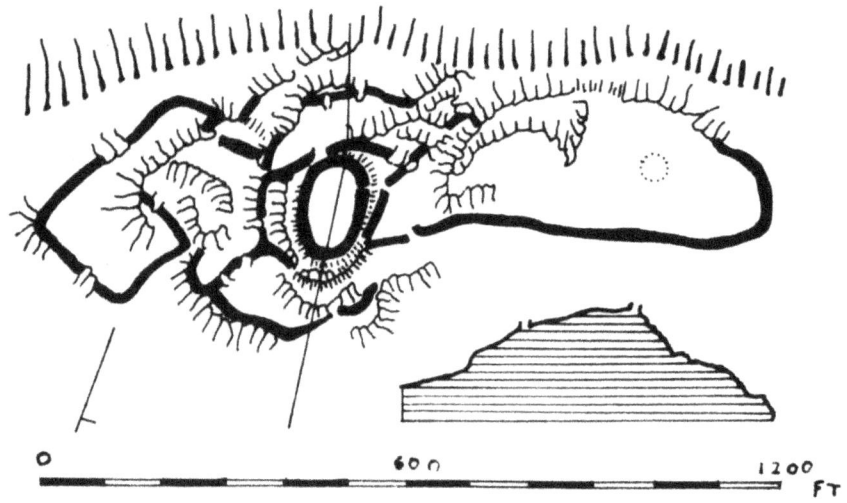

Fig. 3.   Dalmahoy

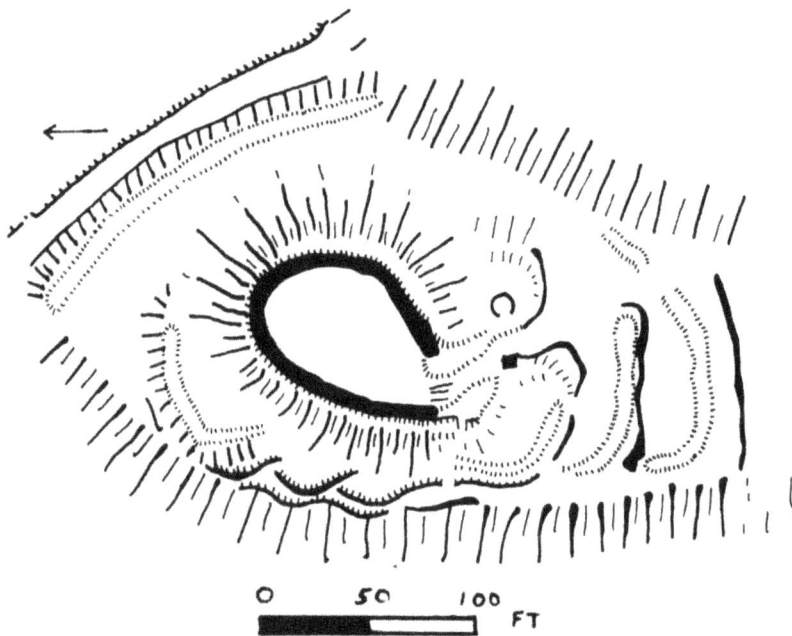

Fig. 4.   Trusty's Hill

centuries B.C. but their origins are far from clear as Clarke has recently pointed out (Clarke, 1971, 30-33). What is certain is that such pins were being used to decorate pottery in the Hebrides in the Early Christian period (Young, 1967, 55; Young, 1952-3, 92), as evinced by a Norse-period ringed pin from the Eye peninsula, Lewis, which has been used to decorate pots in the same manner as that in which projecting headed pins were normally used (Young, 1952-3, Pl.IX, 4). It also should be noted that the Dunadd pin is not bent from a spiral of wire but in a one-piece casting, which marks it out as an elaboration of the basic Iron Age type. Craw suggested that two iron objects with sockets were of Iron Age date, and suggested Continental La Tène parallels for them (Craw, 1929-30, 117). They could, however, simply be larger versions of the Irish socketed and pronged tools, one of which has been found at Dunadd (Craw, 1929-30, Fig. 5,7). The latest finds from Dunadd are Hiberno-Norse, and consist of a trial piece for a penannular brooch of a distinctive type, recently discussed by Graham Campbell (Graham Campbell, 1972), and another trial piece with a design on it in Ringerike style (Christison, 1904-5, Figs. 30-31). Imported pottery from the site is of Thomas' Classes D, E and F, of which Class D is the most diagnostic as it appears to have been current in Gaul in the fifth to sixth centuries (Laing, 1975, 272 for a convenient summary). The clay moulds from the site are also useful, as they include a possible mould for a Class G penannular brooch, a sub-Roman type current in the fifth to sixth centuries (Fowler, 1963, 141), one for a brooch of Class D7 (Fowler, 1963, Fig. 4,6) which is also a sub-Roman type, and what appears to be a mould for an Irish type of F3 brooch current in the late sixth-seventh century (Craw, 1929-30, Fig. 7,6), the Irish counterparts of which are well illustrated by Kilbride-Jones (Kilbride-Jones, 1937). There is thus evidence of occupation in the fifth-sixth century and in the ninth, with a few finds such as the F3 brooch mould, the enamelled interlaced disc (Craw, 1929-30, Fig. 4) and the hand-pin (Christison, 1904-5, Fig. 50) showing that occupation continued on the site during the seventh century at least.

In addition to these listed citadel forts there are several others. A smaller stone-walled 'citadel' enclosure was built in the post-Roman period (from the evidence of finds) at Garn Boduan, Caernarvonshire (Hogg, 1960, 10). The site of Dinas Emrys in the same county utilizes rock outcrops for its defensive scheme, though it lacks a citadel proper. Rocky outcrops were frequently utilized in the post-Roman period - witness Dumbarton Rock, the stronghold of the Strathclyde Britons, the castle rocks in Edinburgh and Stirling or the rock on which the Mote of Mark stands. The citadel site of Clatchard's Craig, Fife, was shown on excavation to have been occupied mainly in the Pictish period (Alcock, 1971, 276-7), and if further evidence of the post-Roman date of Dalmahoy is required it might be pointed out again that it stands adjacent to the large Iron Age hillfort at Kaimes Law, which excavation has recently shown to have been occupied from possibly the late Bronze Age (as suggested by radiocarbon dating) until the Roman Iron Age (Childe, 1940-41, 54; Simpson, 1969). It is difficult to believe that two hillforts would have existed so close to one another at the same period of time.

5

A group of small forts, some of them vitrified, are in the nuclear fort tradition. They are concentrated in Kirkcudbrightshire, and the type site for the series is <u>Trusty's Hill</u>, Anwoth, (Fig. 4) well-known for its Pictish symbol engravings and excavated without diagnostic finds (Thomas, 1961). It was originally suggested, on the strength of a rotary quern and the belief that vitrified forts were invariably of Iron Age date, that the site was first occupied in the second or first century A.D. (Thomas, 1961), and the site was interpreted as consisting of a rampart on the hilltop of stone-built construction and a subsidiary bank and ditch furnished with a guard hut blocking off the north-eastern approach, to which were added in the post-Roman period a series of outlying ramparts and an extension of the original fort entrance with out-turned banks. These works used outer revetments with rubble make-up behind, a technique common in ecclesiastical and secular valla and ramparts in the Early Christian period. Lean-to timber huts, which may have been fired and caused the main rampart to vitrify, were believed to have been contemporary with this secondary phase (Laing, 1975, 33). It is probably no longer necessary to interpret the site as a two-period construction, though this remains a possibility. The excavations at the Mote of Mark have shown that timber-laced ramparts are a feature of the post-Roman period as well as of the Iron Age, and rotary querns once introduced remained the basic quern type during the Early Christian period.

In the same category as Trusty's Hill is <u>Castlegower</u>, Kirkcudbright, which consists of an oval 'citadel' with vitrified rampart enclosing an area about 125 ft by 50 ft (40 m by 16 m), beyond which lie a series of outworks. Similar too is <u>Twynholm</u> (Campbeltown Mote), which has a stone-built citadel about 90 ft by 50 ft (30 m by 16 m) and a similar series of outworks especially to the north and south. Even more closely comparable with Trusty's Hill is <u>Barnheugh</u>, also furnished with a citadel (120 ft by 75 ft, 40 m by 25 m), a stone rampart and dual earthworks. Three circular stone huts can be distinguished on this site. <u>Stroanfeggan</u>, has a citadel (140 ft by 125 ft, 47 m by 42 m) and a complex of outworks. The same pattern is repeated at <u>Edgarton</u>, where the vitrified rampart forms a citadel about 75 ft by 45 ft (25 m by 15 m), and the outworks are also complex.

DEFENSIVE ENCLOSURES

The term 'defensive enclosure' was devised by Feachem to describe a series of 'citadel' forts which are related to nuclear forts by having a small citadel or other stone-walled enclosure within a scheme of outer earthworks (Feachem, 1966, 82-3). Unlike the nuclear forts, which are probably single-period structures, the 'defensive enclosures' are usually Iron Age forts within which 'citadels' have been constructed, and the outworks do not necessarily utilize rock outcrops.

Positive dating for these structures is difficult to establish, but there is no doubt that they are late in the sequence of hillfort development. In a number of cases, for example Craigie Hill, Moncrieffe Hill, Norman's Law,

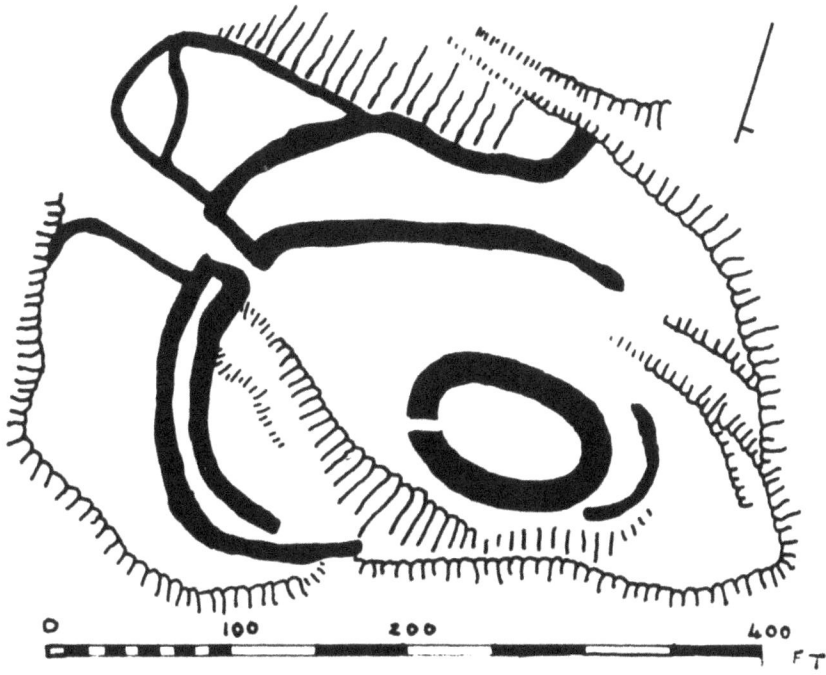

Fig. 5.   Dumyat

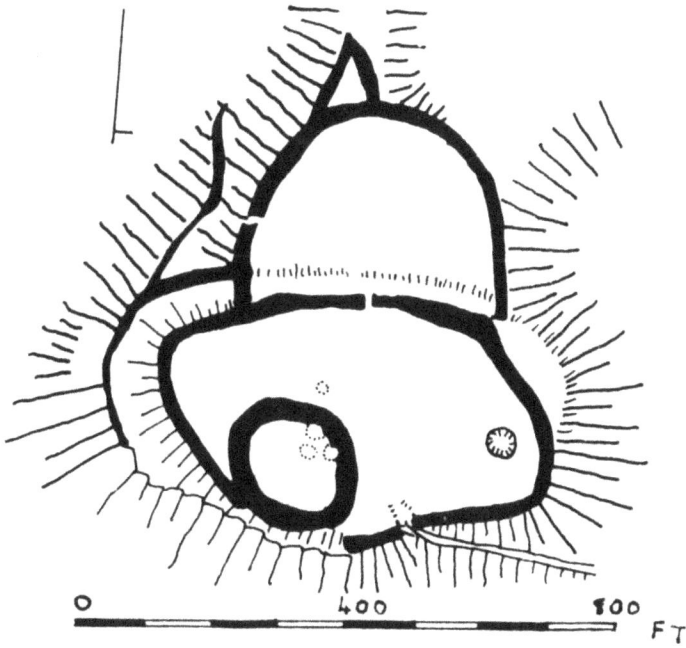

Fig. 6.   Moncrieffe Hill

Dunearn, Carman, Shaw Craigs and Whiteside Rig, and also possibly at Green Craig and Dumyat,(Fig. 5) the citadels were erected on top of existing defences (Feachem, 1966, 84). Ruberslaw, taken by Stevenson to be a true nuclear fort, has much in common with these defensive enclosures, for the citadel is not directly connected with the outer enclosure, which is formed of a single rampart low down the hill. It provides some limited dating evidence since the citadel incorporates re-used Roman masonry, possibly from a signal tower, which implies a date after 200 A.D. (Feachem, 1963, 153). A few sites have stone-walled huts associated with the citadels, for example Moncrieffe, Norman's Law and Carman (Feachem, 1966, 84), and such stone huts are known not to have replaced timber-framed types before the Roman period. Stone huts however are not by any means confined to the Roman Iron Age, and post-Roman examples are known from Crock Cleugh, Roxburghshire (Steer & Keeney, 1946-7), and Huckhoe, Northumberland (Jobey, 1959, 258), where the evidence for post-Roman occupation is provided both by radiocarbon dating and a sherd of F Ware (Thomas, 1959, 100). It should be noted however that while the fort on Humbleton Hill, Roxburghshire, is in many respects a classic example of a defensive enclosure (showing some features of nuclear forts in the arrangement of its defences) the visible hut sites within it are timber-framed, hinting at an earlier date. Round timber huts were however constructed in the post-Roman period, and so are not certain indicators of date (Jobey, 1966, 98-9, and Fig. 7).

A group of defensive enclosures is distributed in Pictland. Of these Moncrieffe Hill, Perthshire, (Fig. 6) is the most noteworthy. Here the first defences consisted of a stone wall following the edge of the hill, converting it into a contour fort. Subsidiary to this is a stone citadel, about 160 ft by 120 ft (43 m by 40 m), probably contemporary with the building of an outer courtyard. Moncrieffe is probably the 'Monad Croib' mentioned as the scene of a battle in 729 (Feachem, 1955, 80). Dumyat, Stirling, (Fig. 5) has a similar citadel with outer defences of regular character (Feachem, 1955, 77). The site on Turin Hill, Angus, (Fig. 7) is a complex multi-period structure, with a stone built citadel inside an oval fortification of vitrified fort type which in turn lies within an oval bivallate fort (Feachem, 1955, 74; Henderson, 1967, 26). The Mither Tap of Bennachie, Aberdeenshire, is a granite tor encircled with defences which merge into the landscape. The outer defence encircles the lower slopes of the tor, while a second encircles the summit (Feachem, 1963, 104). At Dunearn, Fife, (Fig. 8) a dun is set within and partly on top of the inner rampart of a small fort, the rampart being apparently ruinous before the citadel dun was constructed, but possibly being refurbished where necessary (Feachem, 1955, 75). At Tillicoultry, Clackmannan, a citadel of dun shape with meticulously constructed walls is set within a complex of stone built outworks, probably of contemporary date (Feachem, 1955, 73).

In all, there are over a hundred such sites in Scotland. They have no localized distribution, and occur in all areas where Iron Age hillforts are found.

8

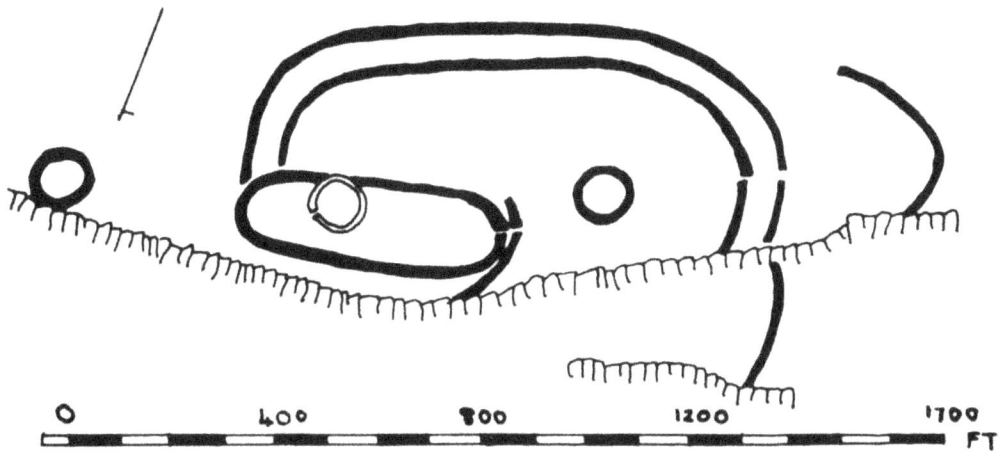

Fig. 7.   Turin Hill

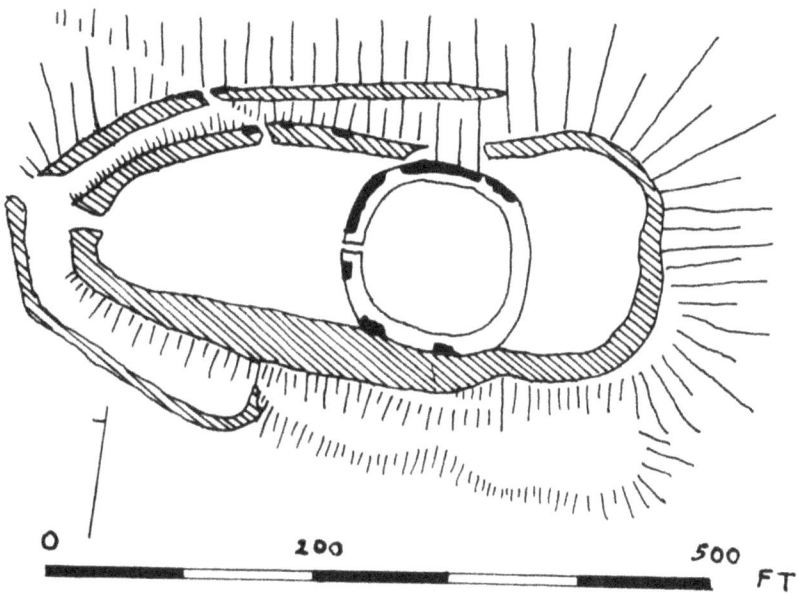

Fig. 8.   Dunearn

HILLFORTS OF OTHER TYPES WITH EARLY
CHRISTIAN OCCUPATION

A few forts appear to have been constructed entirely with timber-laced ramparts in the Early Christian period. Typical of these is the <u>Mote of Mark</u>, excavated by Curle in 1913 (Curle, 1913-14) and re-excavated by the writer in 1973. The occupation was shown to have extended from the later fifth century A.D. until the early seventh, with possibly some later occupation (Laing, 1973; Laing, 1975). The use of timber-lacing is not peculiar to Scotland but occurs in the post-Roman defensive scheme at Cadbury-Camelot (Alcock, 1972, 175-6).

The final phase of the defences of <u>Traprain Law</u>, East Lothian, can probably be ascribed to the fifth century, if not the end of the fourth. Here Bersu's excavations of 1947-8 showed that the final defenses consisted of a stone-faced, turf-cored rampart, about 12 ft (4 m) thick, enclosing 30 acres (13 ha) (Feachem, 1955-56, 289). Bersu demonstrated that the terrace rampart immediately underlying this was constructed about 300 A.D. (<u>Arch. N.L.</u> 1,5(1948),12) and suggested that the final defence was Dark Age. Feachem suggested that it need not be, and could be the work of the fourth century (Feachem, 1955-56, 289), pointing out that there were few finds to suggest post-Roman occupation, although the documentary evidence implies the site was occupied until at least 600. Burley was more in favour of a Dark Age occupation (Burley, 1955-56, 142-3) but could only cite a silver chain of Pictish type as archaeological evidence, seemingly overlooking the mould for a hand-pin of evolved (presumably seventh-century) type from Curle's excavations of 1914 (Curle, 1914-15, Fig.39,4) and the other moulds of post-Roman type, triangular crucibles, ingot moulds and other finds of fifth to seventh century type from the same excavations (Curle, 1914-15, 191-5).

At <u>Hownam Law</u>, Roxburgh, the final phase of occupation consisted of a homestead which partly overlay the ramparts of the earlier fort. The finds suggest a date during the Roman Iron Age for this hut, but it could be later (Piggott, 1947-8, 212) and an iron knife of Early Christian period type was found in the robbing of the Phase II gateway of the fort (Piggott, <u>op. cit.</u>, 219-220), indicating some occupation of the site in the post-Roman period.

A few forts appear to have had passage entrances constructed at the end of their occupation, possibly in the post-Roman period. This is the case at <u>Harelaw</u>, East Lothian (<u>Inv.E.Loth.</u> 254) and also at <u>Stobsheil</u> in the same county, where the inner stone rampart may itself be a late feature (<u>Inv.E. Loth.</u> 85). A similar passage way, 21 ft (7 m) long, occurs at <u>Chatto Craig</u>, Roxburgh, (Fig. 9) which has already been cited as a site of the defensive enclosure class. The inner stone-walled enclosure at <u>Peniel Heugh</u>, Roxburgh, has a cross-wall and is undoubtedly later than the bivallate fort in which it is situated (<u>Inv.Rox.</u> 201).

The Iron Age fort at Castlehill, <u>Dalry</u>, Ayrshire, has two phases of occupation, the first in the Roman Iron Age and the second in the post-Roman

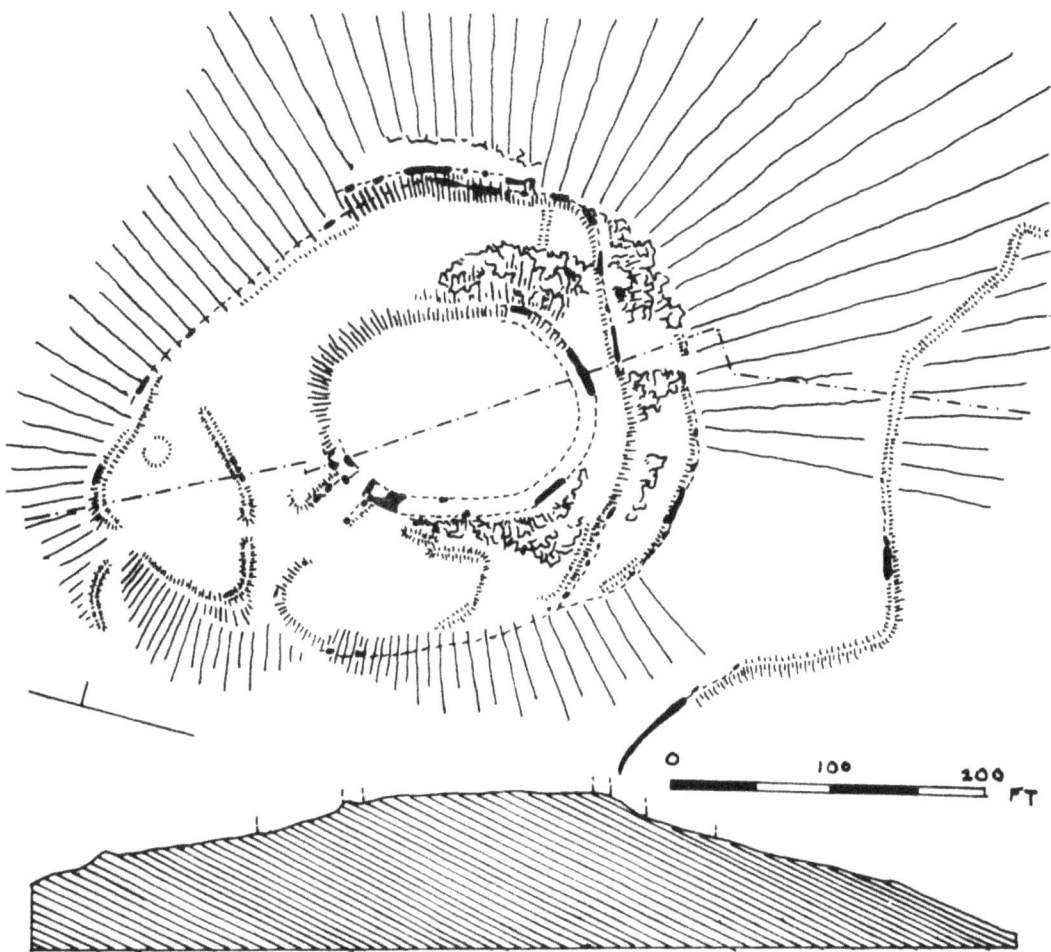

Fig. 9.   Chatto Craig

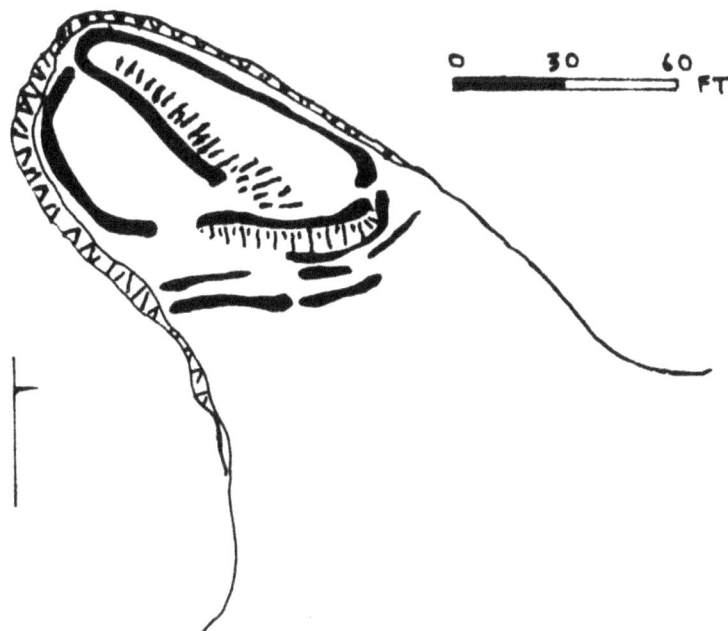

Fig. 10.   Burghead after an 18th-century plan

period, as is suggested by the finding of a brooch of Class G in the penannular series and by other finds (Smith, 1918-19, Fig.4, no.2, and pp.127-8).

In Pictland, a few forts have produced evidence for re-occupation in the Early Christian period. The classic site is Burghead, Moray, (Fig.10) which has produced late Roman coins and a series of Pictish sculptured stones. Here the upper fort was constructed possibly in the fourth century A.D. to judge by radiocarbon dating, and the lower fort was constructed slightly later. The ramparts were timber laced, and finds indicate occupation continuing until the arrival of the Norse (Small, 1969; Laing, 1975, 68-9).

Cullykhan, Banff, is another timber-laced fort with re-occupation. Much of the Pictish occupation material on this site was unfortunately destroyed by medieval castle builders, but a complex of post-holes was interpreted as a rectangular house with porch and has been radiocarbon dated to c.A.D.370 (Grieg, 1972,231; Laing, 1975, 68).

Craig Phadrig, Inverness, is a vitrified fort occupied, on radiocarbon dating evidence, in the fourth century B.C. and subsequently abandoned until the Early Christian period. A radiocarbon date of c.370 was obtained for the Pictish occupation, which was attested by imported E Ware, by a mould for a hanging bowl escutcheon and other small finds. Structural remains included the clay floor of one hut and various hearths (Small, 1971; Laing, 1975, 68).

DUNS

The term 'dun' embraces a diversity of stone-walled forts, characterized by thick walls and the relatively small area of the interior. The sites can conveniently be divided into galleried and ungalleried duns, though distinguishing them can be difficult in some cases (Maxwell, 1969, for discussion). In general terms, they are all offshoots of the general 'castle complex' defined by Childe, characteristic of the Atlantic province, and are regarded by MacKie as having developed around the first century A.D. out of the stone-fort tradition of the Atlantic Iron Age (MacKie, 1965, 105f.), though some timber-laced duns, such as the classic site of Rahoy, seem to date from the beginning of the Scottish Iron Age (MacKie, 1969, 15, for the radiocarbon date; MacKie, 1970, 28-9, for convenient discussion of origins).

While it cannot be doubted that most duns belong to the first two centuries A.D. there are a number which have produced evidence for occupation in the Early Christian period.

The first group is found in Argyll, in the area of historical Dalriada. Here three sites have Early Christian occupation. At Kildonan (Fig. 11) the dun had a stone-built wall 14 ft (3.5 m) thick at its widest point enclosing a roughly triangular area some 63 ft by 42 ft (30 m by 13 m) across. The wall appears to have been constructed by first building a wall of half the thickness of the final defence, with a construction involving outer facing revetments and an inner rubble core. Various intra-mural features were then constructed, notably an intra-mural cell and staircases, and finally the gaps between these features were filled up and the inner wall was faced. The fort was entered by a narrow passage ending with a trip step, at the end of which was a guard-chamber furnished with a hearth. This entrance arrangement seems to have been a secondary modification of a simple passage with door checks and barhole, the original width being reduced by additional masonry. Within the fort were small, roughly circular huts and areas of rough paving (Fairhurst, 1938-9). Finds from the site included a penannular brooch of late sixth-early seventh century date. Nearby was excavated the stack fort of Ugadale Point, which utilized a natural rock stack for part of its defence (Fairhurst, 1954-6). Early Christian period finds included fragments of moulds. Thirdly, Ardifuar (Fig.12) has produced ingot moulds and a crucible of Early Christian type (Christison, 1904-5, 269) but appears to have been initially built and occupied in the first or second century A.D.

In the Hebrides, the galleried dun at Dun Cuier, Barra, (Fig.13) has produced extensive evidence of Early Christian period occupation in the fifth-sixth centuries A.D. The dun utilized the natural rock surface, and consisted of three separate walls, the outer, inner and main walls, pierced by a paved entrance passage way. The finds included a decorated bone comb and baggy, undecorated pottery (Young, 1955-56, 303; Laing, 1975, 86-7). Dun Cuier is of some significance because it was suggested in the report that the baggy, undecorated pottery was the result of Irish influence from Dalriada, and it was compared to the Ulster grass-marked pottery (Young, 1955-56, 311-12), notably that from Larriban. Since pottery of Dun Cuier type occurs on a number of Hebridean sites its chronology and origins are of some relevance. The association of a rim of Dun Cuier type with a mushroom-headed pin of the fifth-sixth century at Sliganach, Kildonan, S.Uist (Laing, to be published) would seem to confirm the Early Christian period date, but there are a number of objections to the suggestion that it is of Irish (Dalriadan) derivation. The main objection to its Irish derivation is that it is grass tempered, not grass marked, and that comparable material is lacking from Dalriada itself (Laing, 1975, 87 and 283). The belief that the Dun Cuier pottery was Dalriadan led to the suggestion that the Hebridean galleried duns were the outcome of Dalriadan expansion, perhaps initially built as a defence against incoming Irish (Young, 1961-62, 198), an idea which was originally propounded by Christison (Christison, 1898, 382-3) who suggested that duns were built by the Dalriadic Scots. There is nothing to support or disprove that the reoccupation of duns may have been contemporary with Dalriadan expansion. There is evidence, including finds of earlier date from several sites, to suggest that duns were already well established before the foundation of Dalriada.

Of the duns that can be equated with Dun Cuier, Bahn, Barra, has produced similar pottery, but is more in the nature of a promontory fort than a dun (Young, 1961-2, 193). Dun Scurrival, also on Barra, has produced Dun Cuier type pottery (Young, 1955-56, 293). A site with similar pottery is Clettraval (Scott, 1948, 46), where the Dun Cuier pottery clearly belonged to a secondary

continued on p. 16

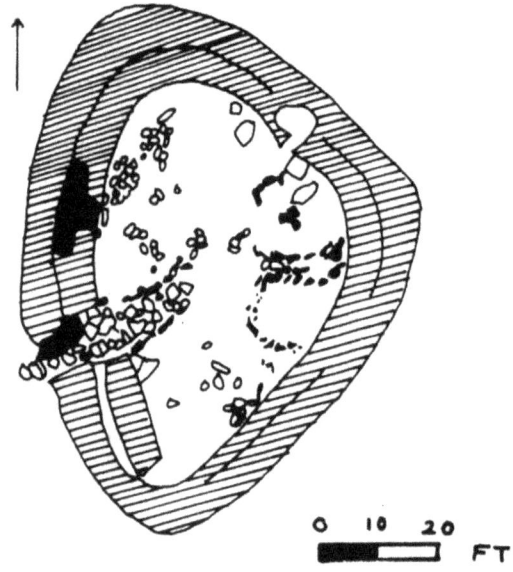

Fig. 11.   Kildonan

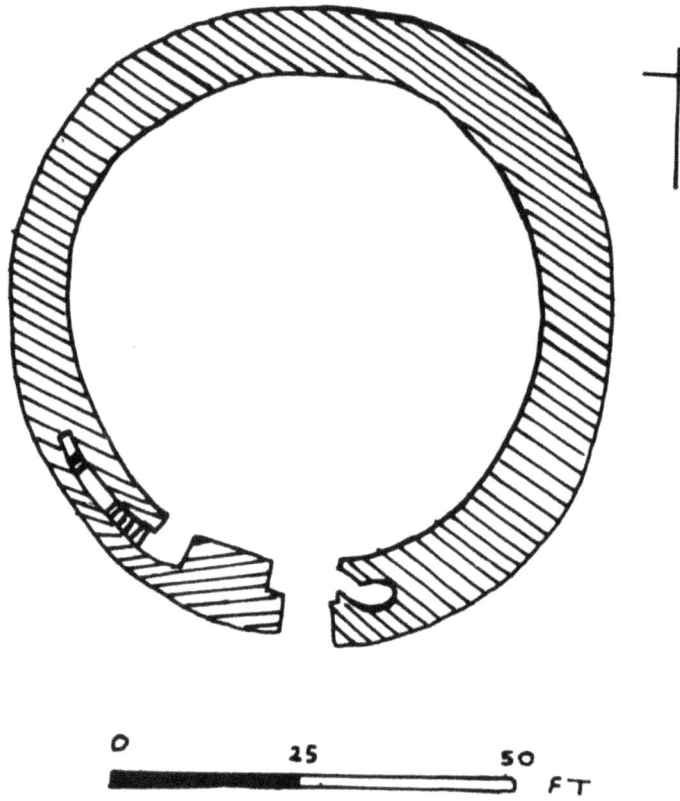

Fig. 12.   Ardifuar

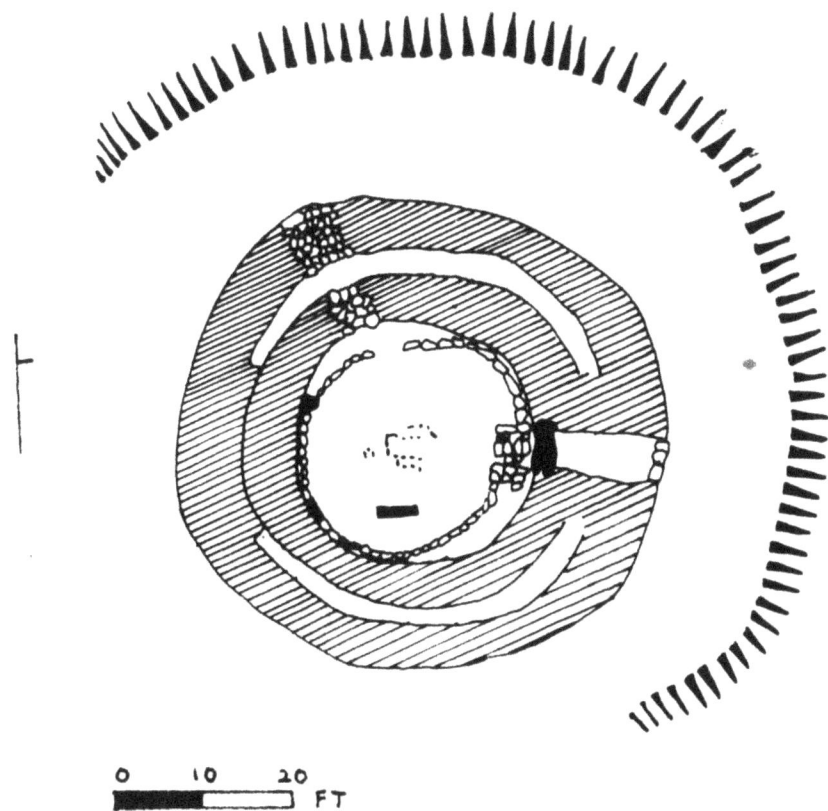

0   10   20
FT

Fig. 13.   Dun Cuier

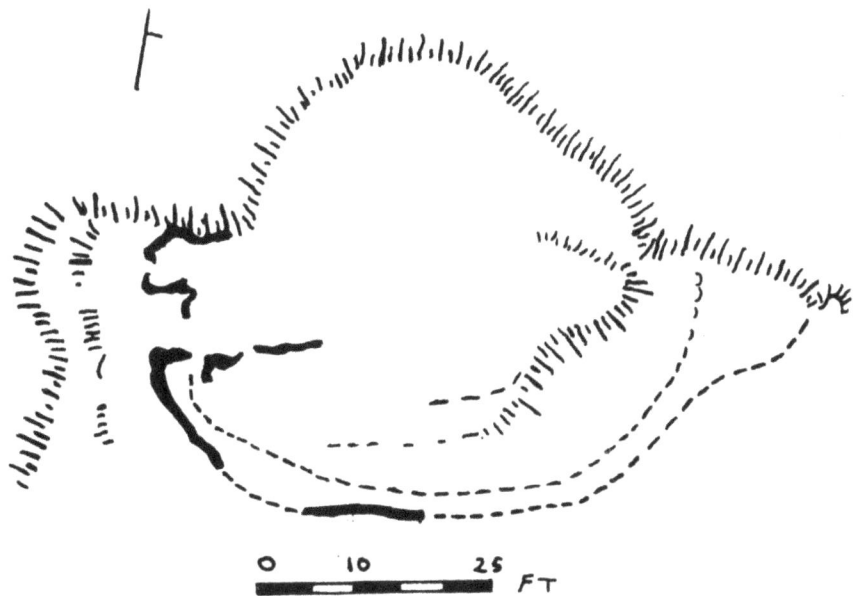

0   10   25
FT

Fig. 14.   An Caisteal

occupation. It was also represented at a'Cheardach Mhor (see below).

A group of Hebridean duns are related structurally to Dun Cuier. These include Tirefuir, Argyll (Young, 1961-62, 190), Caisteal Grugaig, Ross and Cromarty (Young, 1961-62, 189), Ca an Duin, Sutherland (Young, 1961-62, 188) and Dun Ringill, Loch Slapin, Skye.

The puzzling site of An Caisteal, Mull, (Fig.14) seems to combine features of both duns and defensive enclosures (Fairhurst, 1961-2, 107). Although the finds were not diagnostic they would be in keeping with a date in the Early Christian period.

In Southern Scotland, only one dun has produced evidence for re-occupation. This is the site of Castlehaven, Kirkcudbrightshire, which is a galleried, stone-walled fort, 60 ft by 35 ft (20 m by 11 m) in diameter, with a sub-rectangular plan. The finds include a penannular brooch and a blue bead with white trail of Early Christian type (Barbour, 1906-7). Possibly of Early Christian date is the galleried dun at Kilpatrick, Arran (often called the 'cashel'), erroneously identified by Balfour as an Early Christian monastery (Balfour, 1910, 195-206).

ATLANTIC SETTLEMENTS OTHER THAN DUNS

In the Atlantic regions of Scotland, brochs ceased to be built in the first or second century A.D. and were replaced by settlements of various types of smaller, stone-built huts, usually on the site of ruined brochs which were pillaged for stone and which were sometimes re-used by being divided up with stone partitions to form smaller habitation areas (general discussion in MacKie, 1965, 129; Laing, 1974, 126f.). This process was already under way by the end of the second century, as is shown by finds of Roman pottery and other Roman material including coins from post-broch structures (MacKie, 1965, 138-9). In Shetland the main settlement type is the wheel-house, which spread from there to the Hebrides. In Orkney and the north Scottish mainland the wheelhouse is absent, but its place is taken by a type of courtyard house in some ways reminiscent of those in use in the pre-broch period.

It is not easy to determine how late the post-broch settlements were occupied. In Shetland at Jarlshof the occupation of wheelhouses continued until the arrival of the Norse. This is demonstrated by the fact that Norse objects were mixed up with late wheelhouse period finds in middens (Hamilton, 1956, 129), while belonging to the wheelhouse phase at Jarlshof were a Pictish symbol stone and a cross-incised stone (Hamilton, 1956, 84). The broch sites of Orkney and the North Mainland have produced in their final phases finds of Early Christian date. Unfortunately, most of the sites producing diagnostic finds were excavated in the nineteenth century without regard for stratification, and the nature of the Early Christian period occupation is not always easy to determine. The most recurrent artefacts which appear to be intrusive in the fifth-sixth centuries are bone pins, mainly of ball, bead and nail-headed types (discussed in Stevenson, 1955). Broch

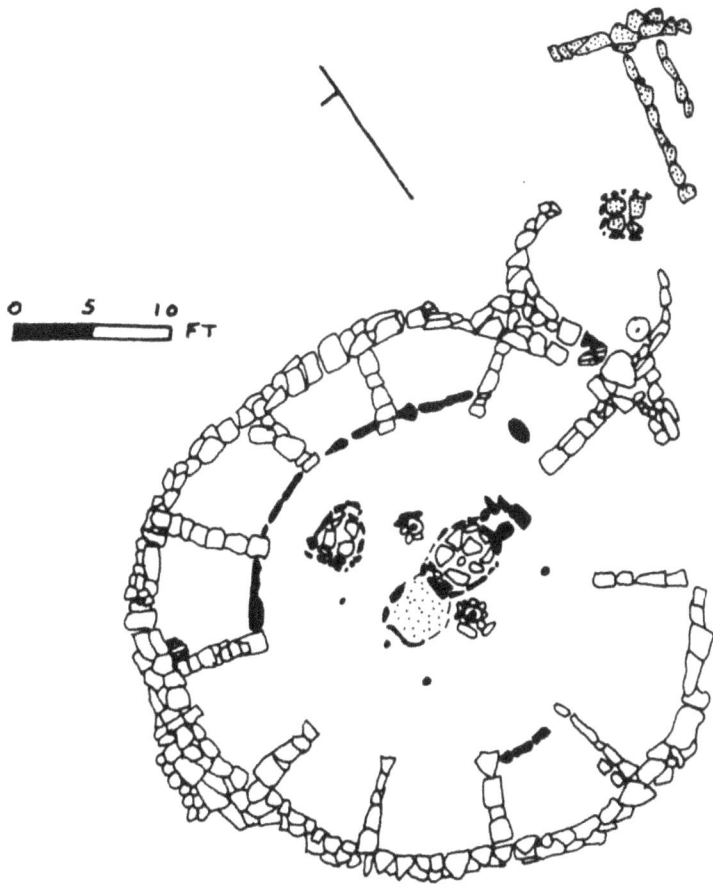

Fig. 15.   a' Cheardach Mhor

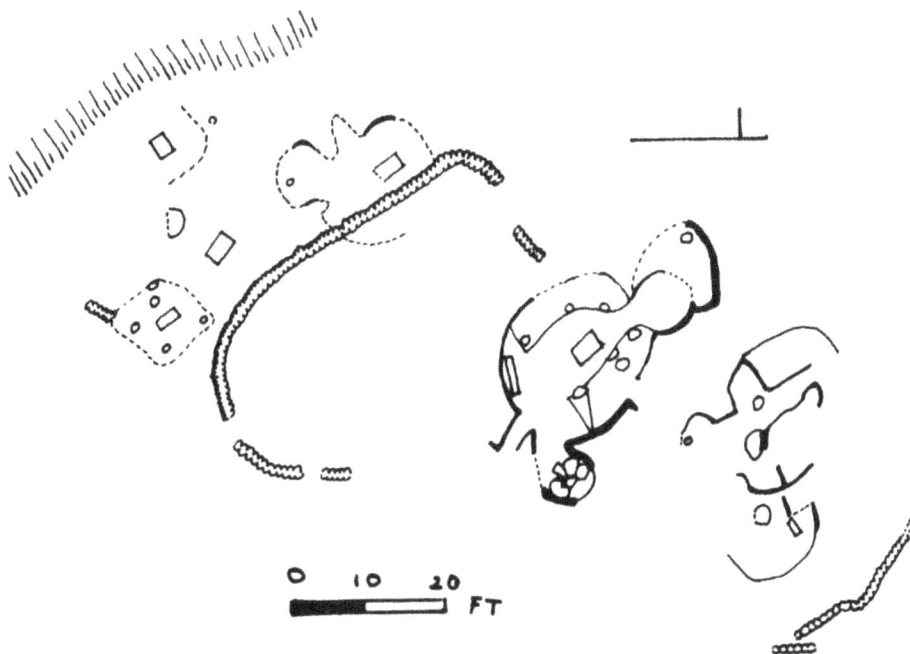

Fig. 16   Udal

sites have produced composite bone combs, triangular crucibles, penannular brooches or bronze stick pins, and also Pictish symbol stones or bones. The Broch of Gurness, Aikerness, produced a penannular brooch of Class F (Kilbride-Jones, 1935-6, 138); the Broch of Burrian, pins, combs and a bone with Pictish symbols (Stevenson, 1955, 283); the Broch of Burray, pins (Stevenson, 1955, Fig.A); Keiss, Caithness, an Irish slotted iron object of Early Christian date (Stevenson, 1955, 285); and the Broch of Oxtro, a symbol stone (Ritchie, 1968-9, 132).

The pattern is repeated in the Hebrides. The site of a' Cheardach Mhor, (Fig.15) Barra, is a typical Hebridean wheelhouse, which appears to have been re-occupied when it was already ruined, a hut being erected from robbed slabs within the wheelhouse. An associated ringed pin, a bone pin and a sherd of what is probably Class B amphora, imply a sixth century date for the re-occupation. This probably continued later as evinced by a scatter of finds, including a composite bone comb and an iron knife of Early Christian type (Young & Richardson, 1959-60, 157). From Bac Mhic Connain came a knife handle with a Pictish ogham inscription (Callander, 1931-2, 65) while from Foshigarry came a composite bone comb with ring-and-dot decoration and some bone pins of Early Christian type (Beveridge, 1930-31, 312). From Sithean a Phiobaire, S.Uist, came a series of bone pins (Lethbridge, 1952, 184).

Two remaining categories of site in Atlantic Scotland show evidence of Early Christian period occupation:

(1) Souterrains, which, though probably in origin Iron Age in the Atlantic province (unless the Bronze Age example at Jarlshof can be considered in the mainstream of souterrain development), seem to have been in use as late as the coming of the Norse. This is implied by Norse literature, which refers to their construction or use in the ninth century in the Hebrides (Orkneyinga Saga, ch.90), and a type of souterrain belongs to the final pre-Norse phase at Jarlshof (Hamilton, 1956, 92).

(2) Figure-of-eight houses are represented in Orkney and in the Hebrides. In the Hebrides they have been excavated at the Udal (Coileagean an Udail), (Fig.16) where the houses consisted of a small circular cell leading from a large ovoid chamber, with one or more turret-like rooms lying along little corridors off the main building (Crawford, 1972, 5-6). The finds included elaborate bone combs, gaming pieces, crucibles, clay moulds, bronze pins and an assortment of other objects, which dated occupation to the period from c.400 till the coming of the Norse (Crawford, loc.cit.). The Orkney site where the same house type occurs is Buckquoy, Birsay, where below three successive Norse houses a sub-rectangular hall leading to a circular chamber was found, which in turn replaced an earlier rectilinear structure built of upright slabs (Laing, 1974, 143). As yet, too few of these houses have been investigated to speculate on their origins.

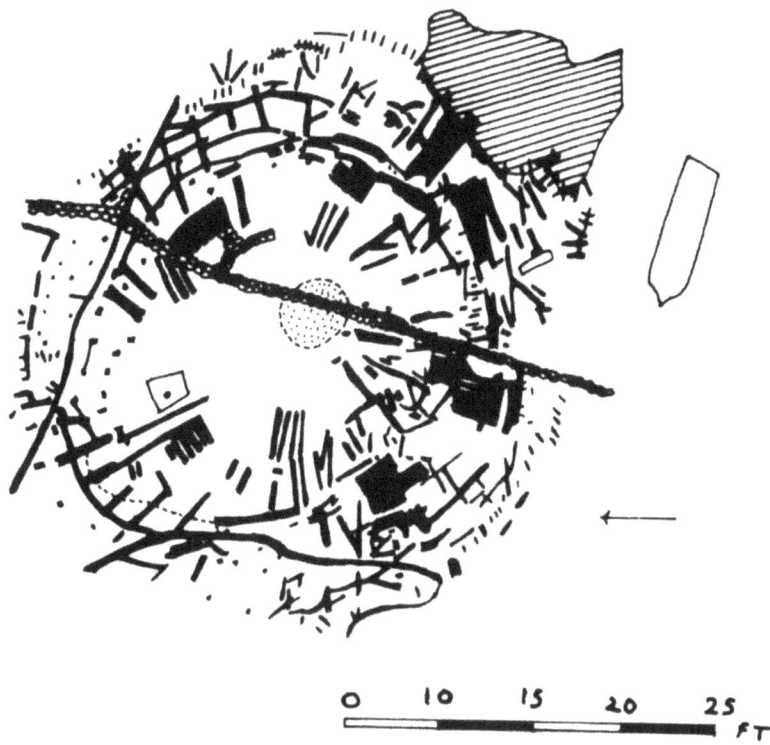

Fig. 17.   Buston crannog

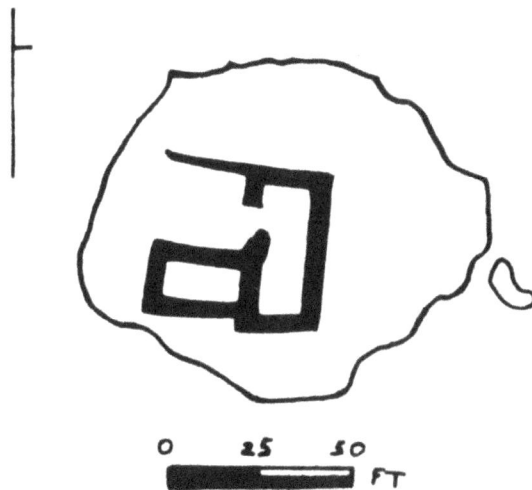

Fig. 18.   Loch Arthur crannog

CRANNOGS

As in Ireland, crannogs or lake dwellings persisted as a settlement type into the post-Roman period. Although some crannogs may have been constructed in Scotland as early as the late Bronze Age, they did not become widespread until the first or second century A.D. With the exception of Milton Loch, Kirkcudbrightshire, few crannogs have been excavated in recent times (Piggott, 1952-3), and the only two crannogs which seem to have been almost exclusively of Early Christian date are not fully published. The first of these is Buston, Ayrshire (Munro, 1882, 190-193), (Fig.17) where dating was provided by imported E Ware and by an ancient forgery of an Anglo-Saxon gold tremissis of the seventh century. The crannog was made up of layers of branches kept in place by rings of piles linked radially and concentrically. An oval house about 50 ft (16 m) at its greatest width with stone and timber walls was constructed on the crannog, but reconstruction is difficult. The finds have been summarized by Laing (Laing, 1975, 37).

The second crannog is that on Loch Glashan, Argyll, excavated in 1960 but not yet fully published (Scott, 1961, 310). Two structural phases were recognized, both probably of the Early Christian period, the earlier being associated with a rectangular timber structure. Occupation was dated to the sixth to ninth centuries by E Ware, a penannular brooch and other finds (summary in Laing, 1975, 76).

Some beads from Dowalton Loch are of Early Christian period type, and may indicate a later occupation of this Roman period crannog (Munro, 1882, 48, Figs.21 and 24). Another crannog in Dowalton Loch has produced an Early Christian period composite bone comb (Munro, 1882, Fig.30). The crannog at Lochlee, Ayrshire, has produced among other finds a ninth-century ringed pin (Munro, 1882, Fig.144), and the crannog at Lochan Dughaill, Argyll, may be of Early Christian origin (Munro, 1892-3, 219). The crannog at Strathcashel Point, Stirling, may also be Early Christian, in view of its proximity to the Early Christian ecclesiastical site (Inv.Stirl. 107).

TIMBER HALLS

I have discussed the phenomenon of the rectangular timber hall in post-Roman Britain in two studies (Laing, 1969; Laing 1975, 132-3), and little more need be said here. I am, however, less confident now that the Angles were not responsible for the introduction of the timber hall into Scotland. With the exception of the unpublished example from Clatchard's Craig, Fife, in Southern Pictland, all the known examples (Doon Hill, Dalry, Kirkconnel) are in areas of Anglian occupation, and Anglian influence is certainly responsible for one at least of the halls at Doon Hill (Hope-Taylor, 1966). In view of the recent early dating for the Anglian occupation at the Mote of Mark (Laing, 1975) it is possible that the hall at Kirkconnel should be reinterpreted as Anglian, or of Anglian derivation.

SECTION II

THE NORSE HOUSE

The arrival of the Norse marks the appearance in Scotland of the longhouse. Norse houses have been excavated at Jarlshof (Hamilton, 1956) and Underhoull (Small, 1964-6) in Shetland, at Birsay (Cruden, 1965; Radford, 1962), Buckquoy (Laing, 1974, 173, following Ritchie, unpublished), Skaill (Laing, 1974, 187), Westness (Laing, 1974, 167) and Orphir (Laing, 1974, 194) in Orkney, Udal (Crawford, 1972; Crawford, 1964) and Drimore (unpublished) in the Hebrides, Freswick (Curle, 1938-9) in Caithness and Dunagoil (Marshall, 1965) in Bute. The general characteristics have been discussed by a number of writers, notably Shetelig (Shetelig, 1954), Small (Small, 1971) and Radford (Radford, 1962). While much has been made in the past of the Norse longhouse as an important factor in the subsequent development of Scottish house plans, in particular the Black House (e.g. by Roussell, 1934), there seems little justification in regarding it as anything other than an intrusive type of dwelling which did not outlive the Norse period.

In general, the Norse houses share certain features in common. The earlier houses have walls with stone facings inside and alternating stone and turf outside, while the later have turf cores faced with stone both inside and out. Flagstones were normally used, but sometimes waterworn boulders from the beach were employed. Roofs were supported on double rows of posts, and stone slabs set on end marked the internal divisions. The setting of the posts for the roofs was irregular, and the construction seems to have involved continuous purlins on each side to carry rafters, the lower ends of which rested on the inner edge of the turf wall. The roofs were of turf, probably on wickerwork with a thatch covering. Generally they measure about 60 ft by 20 ft (20 m by 6.5 m), and are divided into a dwelling room and a kitchen with stone benches running along the walls for beds, etc. Doors are in the short sides, and there is a central hearth. The Norse houses of Scotland are not true longhouses since, in a longhouse, dwelling and byre are under the same roof alignment. In Scotland the stock seems to have been kept in a separate byre, although in Scandinavia the true longhouse is known in the Iron Age. The Norse houses have slightly bowed walls, giving them a boat-shape plan, and appear to be an adaptation peculiar to Scotland of the type of dwelling current in Scandinavia, though related variants occur in both Norway and Iceland. A few, such as Underhoull, were equipped with elaborate drains, (Small, 1964-6, 238), and the associated outbuildings include bathhouses (Curle, 1938-9, 79).

The evidence from three sites is instructive in a consideration of the question of continuity of the Norse house. The first is Jarlshof, where the evidence points to the disappearance of the Norse house in favour of another type of dwelling in the medieval period (Hamilton, 1956, 190). At Jarlshof a small farmstead was built in Norse style but not to a Norse plan in the late thirteenth or fourteenth century. It measured over 63 ft by 20 ft (21 m by 6.5 m) with a small annexe. Later modifications confused the plan, as it was converted into an outhouse or byre. It had an associated barn with a corn-drying kiln in the north-west corner, and probably continued in use until the construction of a tower house in the sixteenth century. The corn-drying kiln attached to the barn is of particular interest since it is circular rather than square, a type also characteristic of Orkney whence it probably spread.

The second site is the Udal, S.Uist, where the evidence both disproves the Viking origin for the Hebridean black house and suggests another antecedent for it. Here building 2 excavated in 1964 has been dated to 1000–1600 A.D. and is of a type seemingly ancestral to the Hebridean black house (Crawford, 1964, 6). The evidence from Udal, where there is a long sequence of Norse occupation extending from the period of the earliest Norse settlements in Scotland, seems to indicate that at the end of the Norse period there was a fairly sharp break in house-building traditions, with the appearance of new types (Crawford, 1965). The development of the Hebridean house has been recently discussed by Crawford suggesting alternative lines of development (Crawford, 1965).

The third site is Little Dunagoil, Bute, where two excavated longhouses could be dated to the period from the twelfth to thirteenth century on the evidence of associated finds, mainly pottery (Marshall, 1965). The Little Dunagoil longhouses have much in common with contemporary structures in the Isle of Man (cf. Gelling, 1957-65; Gelling, 1962-3), and are further from the general type of medieval longhouse than even their earlier Norse antecedents. One had a central row of posts with side aisles (i.e. three rows of roof supports) while the other had a penthouse roof supported on a single row of posts set off centre. Both measured approximately 38 ft by 16 ft (12 m by 5 m).

In Orkney, the available evidence from the current excavations at Skaill, Mainland, suggests a change of house type, though not building traditions, at the end of the Norse period (Laing, 1974, 207, following unpublished information from P. Gelling).

SECTION III

SETTLEMENTS OF IRON AGE TYPE OCCUPIED IN THE
MEDIEVAL PERIOD AND LATER

A variety of native settlement types persisted in Scotland through the Middle Ages and into the post-medieval period. Of these the most note-worthy are crannogs, but duns, hillforts, souterrains, wheelhouses and other Iron Age settlement types were all re-occupied on occasions, and some were modified extensively to suit medieval requirements.

CRANNOGS

Of the various classes of Iron Age settlement, the crannog seems to have been the most persistent, particularly in the West Highlands.

Loch Arthur, New Abbey, Dumfriesshire, (Fig.18) has recently been excavated and appears to be entirely of medieval date (Williams, 1971b). The crannog is about 100 ft (30 m) in diameter, and was approached by a stone causeway about 30 ft (9 m) long. The island was made up of oak piles, driven down in rows, with horizontal beams between. On the island a single building appears to have been constructed with a stone undercroft and timber superstructure - the base of the undercroft originally stood about 36 in (95 cm) high, the walls being of clay bonded construction (almost universal in medieval Scotland) and about 30-36 in (75-95 cm) thick. The main building was 35 ft by 15 ft (11 m by 5 m) and had a cobbled floor. The entrance seems to have been in the long side; at right angles to the main building was an annexe. Although there were no determinate finds from the excavation, a fifteenth century tripod cauldron had been recovered previously from the site. The character of the structures on the island would indicate a late medieval date.

Lochrutton, Dumfriesshire, is another good example of a medieval crannog. Excavated in 1901-2, this structure in Lochrutton Loch appears to have built upon it a hall-house of the mid-thirteenth century (Truckell & Williams, 1967, 141). It was approached by a modified promontory on the eastern shore, and it has been suggested that the whole represents a modifi-cation of the motte and bailey scheme, with the crannog acting as the motte, and the mainland the bailey (Williams, 1971b, 124). Nearly 350 sherds of pottery were found in the excavations, all of the thirteenth to early fourteenth centuries (republished in Truckell & Williams, 1967, 141-8).

Eadarloch, Loch Trieg, Invernesshire, (Fig.19) is a post-medieval crannog which was carefully excavated just before World War II, and from this site it is possible to study the details of construction (Ritchie, 1941-2). The crannog was built on top of an island formed of vegetable matter, mainly pine

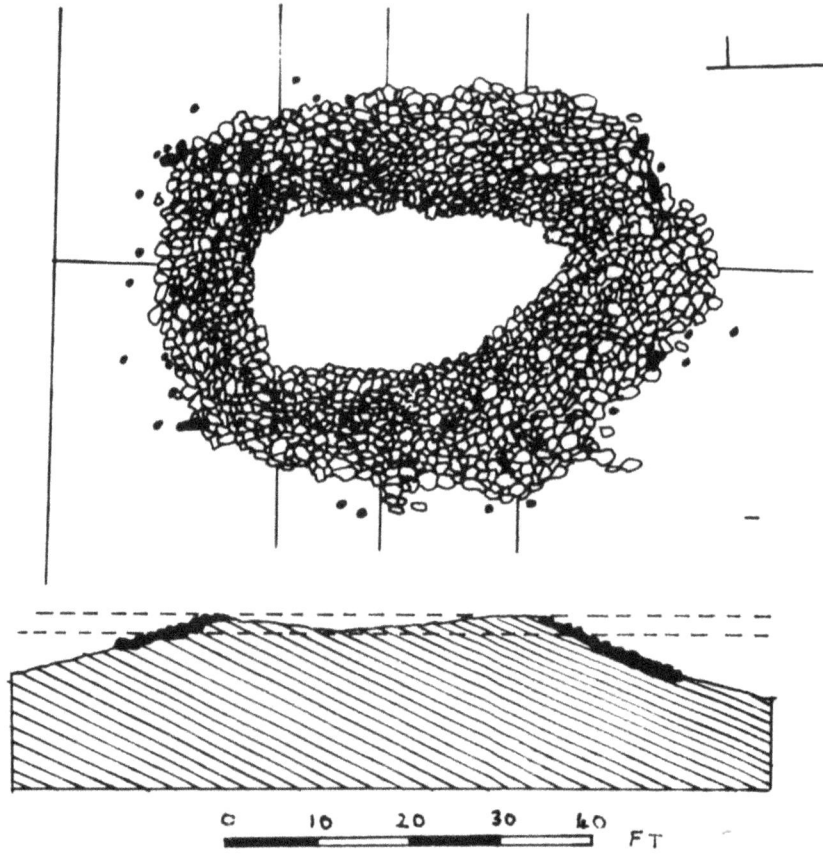

Fig. 19.   Eadarloch crannog

Fig. 20.   Loch of Banchory, crannog house

needles. The construction employed marks an advance on the less stable structures of the Iron Age. First, a layer of brushwood was laid down on which a foundation of large stones mixed with a little earth was deposited. This foundation was hollowed and levelled into the bed of the loch, some 6 to 9 ft (2 to 3 m) under water. In order to work at this depth, it appears likely that a break was made in an adjacent sandbar to drain the area round the site of the proposed crannog, the sandbar being subsequently repaired when the crannog was completed. This restoration of the dam probably proceeded simultaneously with the building of the crannog, so that there was no large-scale flooding at the end. Layers of brushwood were used between layers of timbers or stone and earth in the construction to stabilize it, acting as a kind of 'mortar'. Seven such structural layers were employed, of which a basal layer of timbers, an intermediate layer and an upper platform were the most important. Round the island were piles or stakes, driven in to prevent lateral movement, forming a rectangle in line with the rectangle of the framework. The basal raft was some 65 ft by 45 ft (32 m by 15 m), made of squared beams not less than 6 ft (2 m) apart. The upper platforms were more carefully constructed, the uppermost floor being well woven and employing neat jointing. On top of the wooden framework was a floor of stones, on which were hearths. The dwelling, of which little evidence remained, was oblong, of light timber construction with a central substantial roof support. Finds were fairly plentiful, and indicated an exclusively sixteenth to seventeenth century occupation.

A crannog on Loch Cannor, Aberdeenshire, produced an animal-spouted bronze tripod cauldron (Munro, 1882, Fig. 2-4) datable to the fourteenth century (for the type, see Anderson, 1878-9). This site is documented as having James IV as one of its visitors in 1506, and continued in occupation until 1648, when its destruction was ordered. It is first mentioned in 1335 (Munro, 1882, 21). A tripod cauldron, spouted vessel and two other cooking pots were found on a very large crannog site in the Loch of Banchory, which measured nearly 200 ft by 100 ft (65 m by 32 m) and which had on it the foundations of a stone structure of late medieval date (Munro, 1882, 27 and Fig. 9), (Fig. 20). The site is documented in the sixteenth and seventeenth centuries (Munro, loc. cit.). A crannog at Croy, Invernesshire, appears to have been medieval (Munro, 1882, 31). Loch Barean, Dumfriesshire, has a crannog which has produced medieval cooking pots (Munro, 1882, 38). A crannog at Ledaig, Argyll, produced a wooden comb of a type current in the fifteenth century in Scotland, which is matched by an unpublished example from Caerlaverock Castle, Dumfriesshire (Munro, 1882, 55, for the crannog). A crannog in the Loch of Kilbirnie, Ayrshire, produced a variety of medieval finds, including an iron pot and an animal-shaped manile (Munro, 1882, Fig. 32). The crannog at Lochlee, Ayrshire, obviously had a multi-period occupation, for apart from the Roman and Early Christian period finds it also produced objects of sixteenth or seventeenth century date, such as the brass mounted knife (Munro, 1882, Fig. 133) and a number of other iron implements of similar date (e.g. Munro, 1882, Figs. 127-8). The crannog at Friar's Carse, Dumfriesshire, produced medieval pottery of the late thirteenth century (Munro, 1882, Figs. 160-61), and a key of medieval type (op. cit. Fig. 176; compare L.M.C. Fig. 42, II). Buston crannog,

Ayrshire, has produced a medieval ring brooch of the fourteenth century (Munro, 1882, Fig. 241; compare L.M.C. Pl. LXXVII, 1) while Lochspouts, in the same county, has produced medieval pottery (discussed in Laing, 1974b, 187) and a medieval pendant (Munro, 1882, Fig. 264). A medieval gaming piece was found in a crannog in the Loch of Forfar (Munro, 1882, Fig. 7), and the crannog in Black Loch, Wigtown, is also probably medieval (Inv. Wigt. 32).

In 1608 an act was passed 'That the haill houssis of defence strongholdis and cranokis in the Yllis pertaining to thame and their foirsaidis sal be delyverit to his Maiestie and sic as his Heynes sall appoint to ressave the same to be vst at his Maiesty's pleasour' (Regist. Secreti Concilii: Acta penes Marchiarum et Insularum Ordinem, 1608-1623, pp. 4, 5) and there are numerous references to crannogs in documentary sources from the fourteenth to the seventeenth centuries (see also Crawford, 1967, 89).

A few additional medieval crannogs may be noted. At Lochan Dughaill, Argyll, medieval pottery was found in the nineteenth century (Piggott, 1952-3, 151), while the crannog on Black Loch, Wigtown, also probably had medieval occupation, though it was originally constructed in the first or second century A.D. (Inv. Wigt. 32). Medieval pottery (unpublished) was found in the crannog at Hyndford, Lanark.

The Scottish evidence may conveniently be compared with that from Ireland. A map of Richard Bartlett shows a crannog being attacked in Lough Raughan, Co. Tyrone, at the beginning of the seventeenth century, and presumably depicts an historic capture which was led by Mountjoy in 1602 (Norman & St Joseph, 1969, Fig. 41 and p. 84).

ISLAND SETTLEMENTS

Related to crannogs are island settlements. These appear to be exclusively North British, and are located on small islands in lochs. They usually consist of a small cluster of buildings. Islands were frequently selected for tower houses in medieval Scotland, the most famous examples being Loch Leven Castle, Loch Doon Castle and Threave. These settlements frequently appear to have had an ecclesiastical origin, as was demonstrated in the excavation of the settlement on Loch Glashan (see below), so it is possible that their origins should not be sought in crannog type lacustrine settlement but in the eremitic monasticism of the Early Christian period. The classic Early Christian island chapel site on Ardwall Isle, Kirkcudbright, was replaced by a medieval hall house and subsequently by an eighteenth century inn (Thomas, 1961, 88), and one need not look far for examples of island-sited Celtic ecclesiastical foundations - Iona, Lindisfarne, St. Cuthbert's Isle, Luchubran, St. Ninian's Isle, Sgor Nam Ban-Naomha, Eileach Naomh and Papil, West Burra, are all well-known examples from North Britain (see Thomas, 1971, passim), while medieval priories on islands are well exemplified by Inchcolm Abbey in the Forth.

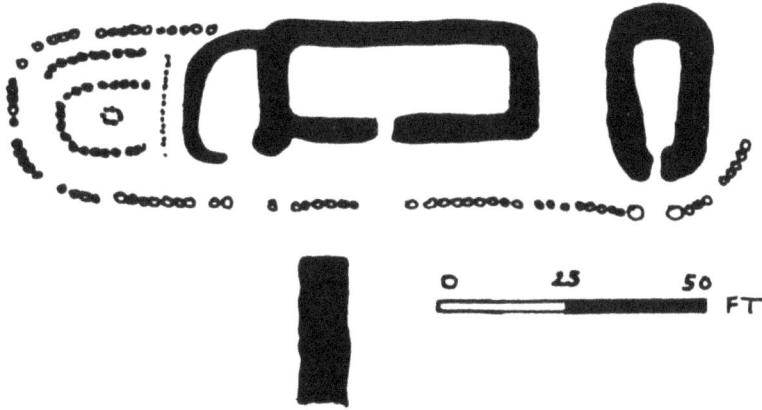

Fig. 21.　Loch Doon houses

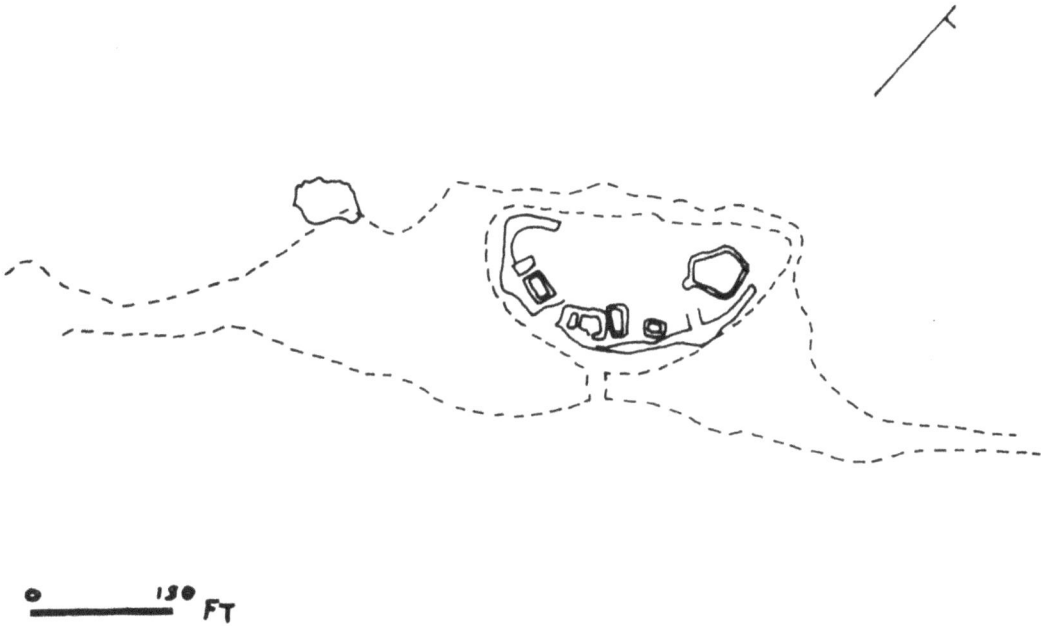

Fig. 22.　Loch Glashan settlement

Two island settlements have been excavated: that in Loch Doon, (Fig. 21) Ayrshire, was connected to the mainland by a causeway. There were an encircling wall and two drystone buildings with a further one of wood (Fairbairn, 1936-7). The larger building was 43 ft by 12 ft (14 m by 4 m), without a hearth. A coin of Edward I and some fourteenth century pottery provided the dating evidence (Fairbairn, 1936-7, 327). The larger building had an entrance in the long side, and an annexe with a separate entrance butted on to it. The smaller building was similarly rectangular but more substantial with walls 8 to 12 ft (2.5 to 4 m) thick, still standing to a height of 4 ft (1.3 m). The entrance was in the gable wall, and at the opposite end was a hearth pit. The interior measured about 8 ft by 6 ft (2.6 m by 2 m). Both structures were roofed with turf, presumably resting on timbers supported by the wall head. The timber structure appears to have been an oval hut, with central roof support, about 15 ft (5 m) in diameter.

The settlement on an island in Loch Glashan, Argyll, (Fig. 22) appears to have been originally planned as an ambitious ecclesiastical settlement, but adapted to a more humble use. It consisted of a small revetted island approached by a causeway, with five buildings, three of which seem to have been in use in the thirteenth-fourteenth century (Fairhurst, 1969, 47f.). One was interpreted as a chapel, the other two as primitive dwellings. All were drystone built, and all originally unicameral, though one had a cross-wall later inserted. Building III was 25 ft by 15 ft (8 m by 5 m) internally, Building II about 35 ft by 17 ft (11 m by 5.5 m). Building I, interpreted as a chapel, was 24 ft by 12 ft 3 in (7.3 m by 3.7 m) with a west doorway. It was better built than the others (Fairhurst, 1969, 54-6).

HILLFORTS

Evidence for medieval occupation within the decayed ramparts of hillforts comes from many parts of Scotland. Hillforts were not infrequently chosen for the site of subsequent castles. At Tynron Doon, Dumfriesshire, the fort which had been re-occupied in the Early Christian period was again re-occupied in the early Middle Ages (when it may have been partly utilized for a motte) and in the sixteenth century a tower house was erected on the site (Williams, 1971a, 108). The medieval castle at Dundonald, Ayrshire, also stands within the earthworks of an earlier hillfort, possibly of Early Christian date. Early Christian too are the probable predecessors of Edinburgh Castle, Stirling Castle, Dumbarton Castle, Dunnottar Castle (Henderson, 1967, 211) and many others of lesser importance. Castle Urquhart, Inverness, and Dunnideer, Aberdeenshire, both have castles set within vitrified forts.

Re-occupation of a different nature can be found within a number of Lowland hillforts, as well as a few in Pictland. Recent excavations at Burghead, Moray, have shown the site to have been occupied in the twelfth to thirteenth century (Small, 1969, 67). The Pictish fort at Cullykhan, Banff, was similarly occupied in the twelfth to thirteenth century, as suggested by pottery and other finds (Grieg, 1972).

Two Renfrewshire forts have produced evidence of farmsteads being established within the existing forts. At Knapps a complex of structures was recognized within an enclosure wall, dated by finds to the fourteenth to fifteenth centuries (Newall, 1965). At Walls Hill the farmstead dated from the thirteenth to fourteenth century, and was a type of longhouse (Newall, 1960).

SOUTERRAINS

Souterrains seem to have been re-used occasionally as byres or stores, presumably attached to medieval farmsteads. Medieval pottery has been found in Wester Yardhouses souterrain, Carnwath, Lanarkshire (unpublished, in National Museum of Antiquities of Scotland), and in or around a number in Angus.

DUNS

Duns were re-occupied intermittently down to the nineteenth century. A number of both Perthshire and Argyllshire duns have within them rectangular buildings, mainly shepherds' huts, of this period, and in the case of one Perthshire dun, Roro, a school (Watson, 1912-13, 39). Without excavation it is almost impossible to date the rectangular buildings found inside duns. Thus the structures inside the dun at Am Baghan Galldair, near Glenelg, Inverness, include two stone-built circular huts, which probably post-date the original construction of the dun, and a further rectangular three-roomed house which is late medieval or post-medieval (Bogle, 1894-5, 184 and Fig. 6). The dun at Loch nan Cinneachan, on Coll, stands on an island attached to the mainland by a causeway. The island is completely surrounded by a wall, within which and adjacent to the dun are a series of rectangular buildings (Beveridge, 1903, 25). In many respects this is similar to the series of island settlements discussed above (p. 26).

A number of duns have produced positive evidence of medieval re-occupation.

Kildonan, Argyll (above, p. 12), was re-occupied in the fourteenth century, as is demonstrated by pottery and other finds. At this period six small round huts were erected with timber framing within the dun, part of the interior being converted into a paved yard (Fairhurst, 1938-9, 207). The gateway was altered slightly, restoring it to its original appearance in the first (Iron Age) occupation phase, and a gallery was filled in, but otherwise no major alterations took place. Medieval pottery of a similar date indicates re-occupation at Dun Fhinn in Kintyre (D. & E. 1966, 11f.), while at Dun Lagaidh (Fig. 23) the recent excavations have shown extensive remodelling. This medieval re-occupation was dated by a coin hoard deposited some time after 1247 (MacKie, 1968, 7), and structural evidence showed that the existing sequence of vitrified fort with overlying dun was modified into a type of castle and bailey, the dun forming the castle and the vitrified fort the bailey (Selkirk,

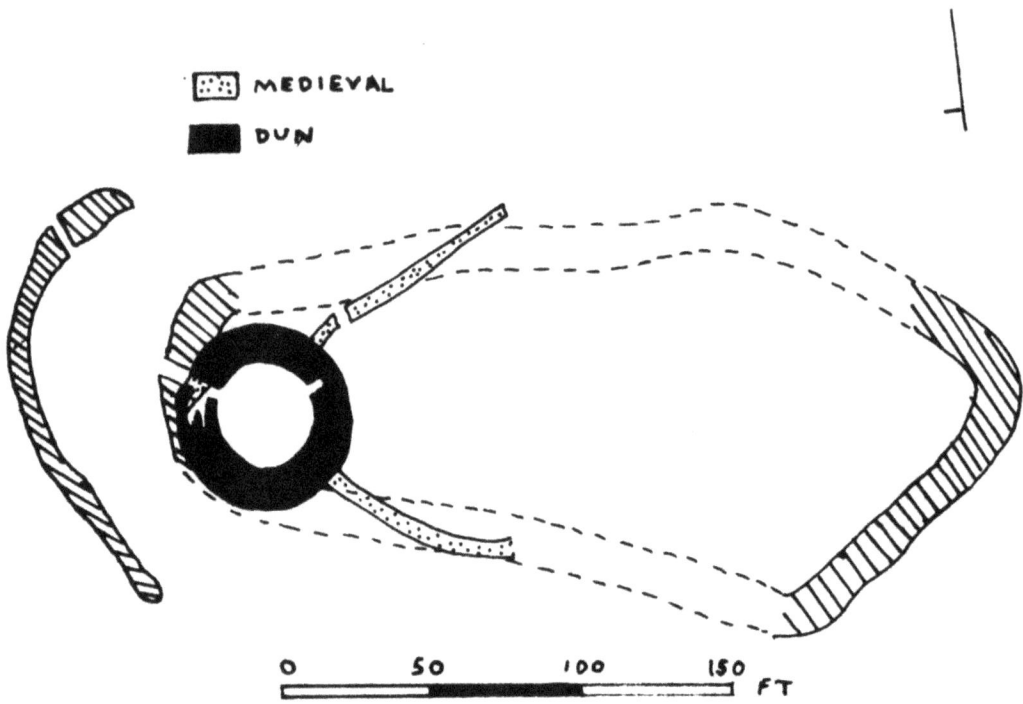

MEDIEVAL

DUN

0   50   100   150 FT

Fig. 23.   Dun Lagaidh

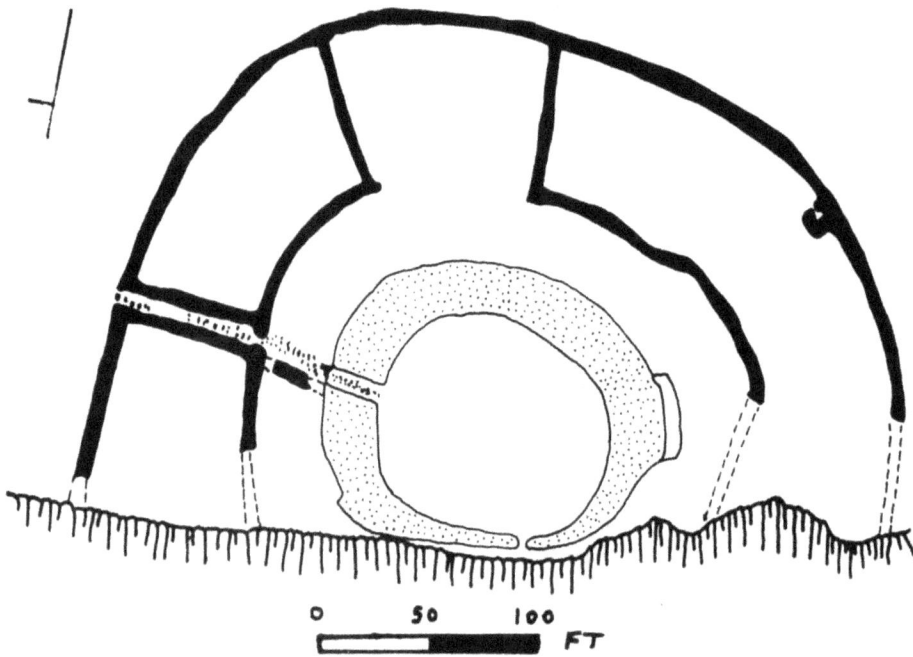

0   50   100 FT

Fig. 24.   Cahercommaun

1969, 11). The entrance to the dun was walled up and masonry constructed along the length of the guardchamber to strengthen the outer wall. The original intra-mural staircase was remodelled as a 'castle' entrance, and radial walls were built to link the dun with the vitrified fort. In the post-medieval period a settlement was established adjacent to the site; excavation of one house site confirmed the local tradition that it was occupied in the 1840s (MacKie, 1968, 8-9).

A dun-like enclosure on Dun Mara, Lewis, has two sub-rectangular houses very similar to degenerate Norse longhouses of the kind that were being built in the twelfth to thirteenth centuries (Mackenzie, 1903-4, 203, Fig. 29). Two sites on Loch Sween, Argyll, appear to have rectilinear buildings of medieval date constructed within them. Dun Mhuirich, Linne Mhuirich, is a structure in many ways reminiscent of nuclear forts. It has an inner, oval citadel with the remains of rectangular structures and an outer enclosure lower down the rock which utilizes the natural outcrop for defence, the outer enclosure however being concentric with the inner. The inner citadel is about 54 ft by 38 ft (16 m by 11.5 m) (Christison, 1904-5, 246-8). The site on Eilean na Circe is of particular interest, since in some respects it belongs to the category of island settlements. The remains consist of an outer enclosure wall, seemingly enclosing most of the island, within which are the remains of rectangular buildings. It should be compared with the settlement on Loch Glashan (Christison, 1904-5, 241-3).

The galleried dun at Dun Cuier, Barra, occupied in the Early Christian period, was again re-occupied in the eighteenth century when a rectangular building was constructed filling the interior. Associated finds included an eighteenth century knife handle and craggan pottery as well as a clay pipe bowl (Young, 1955-56, 294-6).

SCOOPED SETTLEMENTS

Some debate has surrounded the date of the occupation of 'scooped settlements', a class of monument found particularly in the Southern Uplands. One such settlement has been excavated at Manor, Peeblesshire, and has been found to be medieval. The characteristic feature of such settlements is the scarping of a terrace into the hillside for the construction of round timber-framed huts, with or without an outer enclosure (Stevenson, 1942-3, 95-6). The settlement at Manor was found to consist of a cluster of circular huts with roofs supported on more than one post, surrounded by an enclosure wall.

Scooped settlements are distributed in Roxburgh (especially round the Bowmont Water), round the Gala Water near Edinburgh, in Peeblesshire, Berwickshire and Dumfriesshire, where they are known as birrens (Stevenson, 1942-3, 95-6). They average 100-150 ft (30-45 m) across.

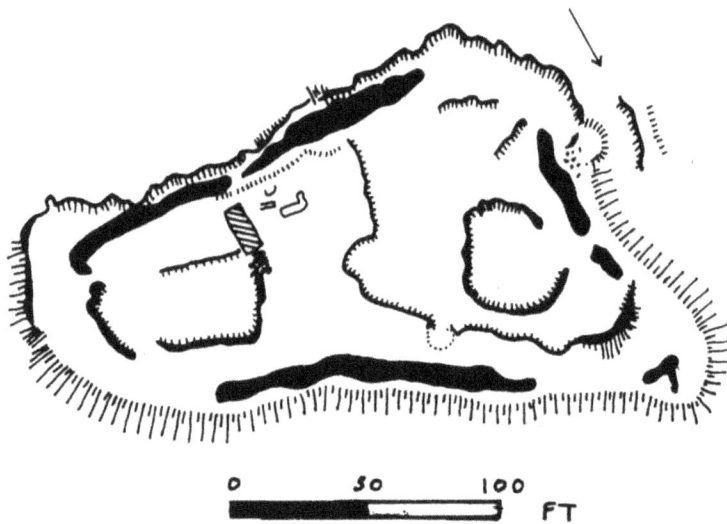

0   50   100
                            FT

Fig. 25.   Mote of Mark

DISCUSSION

From the foregoing survey, one important point emerges. The settlement types of Early Christian Scotland are those of the Iron Age, and there is no category of late Iron Age settlement (i.e. one occupied in the first to second centuries A.D.) that does not appear to have been occupied at least sporadically in the period from the fifth century onwards. It is clear that this settlement pattern was established by the end of the second century, when brochs were being replaced by various categories of stone huts in the Atlantic province and when souterrains in Angus were being replaced by post-souterrain huts. It is to be admitted that the continuity of post-souterrain huts cannot be proved to extend into historical times, but only two such settlements, Carlungie I and Ardestie have been excavated, and neither produced dateable finds. What is clear from those sites is that the souterrain builders and the post-souterrain hut builders were the same people (Wainwright, 1963, 34) just as the round hut builders of Shetland were the same people as the broch builders (Hamilton, 1956, 59), and MacKie has stressed the basic continuity of culture from broch to wheelhouse periods (MacKie, 1965, 129-132). Before the Anglo-Norman penetration of Scotland only two intrusive types of settlement can be recognized: the rectangular timber hall, which does not appear to outlive the seventh century and which had little or no effect on subsequent settlements, and the Norse house which, although widespread in the areas of Norse settlement, also appears to have had little effect on subsequent settlement types in Scotland. The few timber halls known may owe something to the influence of the Anglo-Saxons, and some at least were the work of Anglo-Saxon incomers. If there is continuity of occupation on examples of all classes of Iron Age settlement, can it also be claimed that all categories continued to be built in the post-Roman period, or were the sites occupied simply earlier Iron Age structures with some refurbishings? As this survey has shown, some sites were undoubtedly reoccupied, and finds attest original construction in the first or second century A.D. or even earlier. In each category of monument however there are a few examples which appear to be of entirely post-Roman construction. In the hillfort class, the evidence from Dunadd suggests strongly that nuclear forts are purely a phenomenon of the Early Christian period, while the evidence of the Mote of Mark shows that forts with timber-laced ramparts were being built in the fifth century. The finds from Buston crannog, Ayrshire, show that this site was first occupied in the Early Christian period, though there may have been later use of the site. The finds from the galleried dun at Dun Cuier, Barra, suggest that some Hebridean duns were built for the first time in the fourth century or later, while the finds from a number of post-broch huts show that a few at least were still being built in the Early Christian period.

A consideration of the distribution of sites occupied in the Early Christian period shows that continuity can be observed here too. The distribution of crannogs of Iron Age (i.e. first or second century A.D.) date is not noticeably different from that of crannogs occupied in the post-Roman period; in the areas where forts were common in the Iron age, re-occupied forts are also common; where duns are distinctive, re-occupied duns are to be found.

The continuity of the settlement types themselves is reflected in other ways. One of the most interesting is in the continuity of prehistoric ritual sites into the Christian era, and the way in which the plans of these may have influenced the layout of Early Christian cemetery sites. The subject has been discussed at length by Thomas (Thomas, 1971, 58-66) and stressed by MacKie (MacKie, 1970, 31-2) and need not be elaborated here.

Continuity is also very much apparent in the material culture of the Early Christian Celts. Some of the basic range of equipment would not look out of place on a Bronze Age or even earlier prehistoric site. Flint tools were found at Buston (Munro, 1882, 214) and at Mote of Mark (where they were found to be re-used Mesolithic implements: see Laing, 1973, 123), while bone needles, awls and other such artefacts are recurrent finds on sites of all periods from the neolithic onwards. Blue glass beads of the type represented at Dunadd and elsewhere are also a ubiquitous Iron Age type (MacKie, 1971, 48). So too are the jet or shale bracelets which occur at Mote of Mark, Dunadd, Buston and a variety of Early Christian period sites and on Iron Age sites such as Castlelaw, Midlothian (Henshall, 1955-56, 265), Craig's Quarry, East Lothian (Piggott, 1957-8, 76) and Traprain Law, where they may be Bronze Age (Henshall, 1955-56, 265). They also occur in a Bronze Age context at Heathery Burn, Co. Durham (Henshall, loc. cit.). Stone polishers, whetstones, pounders and rubbers occur at all periods down to the medieval, as do spindle whorls. Spiral finger rings, possibly introduced in the second century B.C. from England (Piggott, 1949-50, 131-4; MacKie, 1969, 25, but see Clarke, 1971, 25-28 for contrary view) continue into the post-Roman period in a slightly different guise, in gold at Buston (Munro, 1882, 229) or silver at Norrie's Law (Anderson, 1881, 34-42). Once established, rotary querns remained in use throughout the Early Christian period (for the Dunadd collection, Christison, 1904-5), while such Early Christian type fossils as penannular brooches (Fowler, 1963), hand-pins (Fowler, 1963, 125f.) and other types of dress fasteners have their origins in the Iron Age even if their immediate prototypes are Romano-British. This list could be greatly extended. For example, ironwork in the Early Christian period often has Iron Age parallels, even if not from Scotland (see Laing, 1975, 285-95 passim). It must of course be added that some types of object are of Roman derivation or appear to have reached Celtic Britain by way of Germanic Migration Period contacts (see the list in Hencken, 1950, 16-17, which analyses the origins of objects from an Irish crannog where the finds are comparable to those in Scotland), but these are not usually objects directly related to the subsistence economics of the community, where the range of equipment can be seen to be remarkably static.

This cultural continuity, apparent in settlement types and in artefact assemblages, is also apparent in socio-historical terms. The growth of Pictland can be traced from the late Bronze Age through to Early Christian times, the Picts being the descendants of the Caledonians and before them the people grouped by MacKie as his Abernethy culture (MacKie, 1970, 20-21), and although the relationship between Scottish animal art of the Iron Age and Pictish art is not perhaps as direct as Thomas would have us believe (Thomas, 1961b), the relationship nevertheless exists. Leaving aside the intrusive cultures of the Irish of Dalriada and the Angles of southern Scotland, the origins of the early British kingdoms of the post-Roman period must be sought in the tribal structure of the Roman Iron Age, as provided by Ptolemy. Thus behind Gododdin lies the tribal territory of the Votadini, behind Rheged lies that of the Novantae, behind Strathclyde (and Aeron?) lies that of the Damnonii. Such tribal divisions, apparent in the formation of the early British kingdoms, are also apparent in the diocesan divisions of the early Church in Southern Scotland, as Thomas has argued (Thomas, 1968, 110-16).

How far this can be projected into the period after 1100 A.D. is difficult to determine. There can be no doubt that the feudalization of Scotland, particularly under David I, had a radical effect at any rate in Lowland Scotland on the pattern of settlement. It led to the growth of villages and towns on the English model, and with them an economy which depended on the burgh as the territorial focus of trade and industry, economically linked to a network of villages and sheilings in the hinterland (Laing, 1969, gives a convenient summary). In the Lowlands, where sites of Iron Age type were re-occupied they served a differing function. Hillforts had the farmsteads of single families set within them, as at Walls Hill or Knapps, and were no longer defensive. Crannogs continued because they were simply an obvious adaptation of a nucleated homestead to a loch-dominated environment, and as such were as valid in a feudal world as in the familiar world of the Celtic clans. Beyond the areas dominated by the Scotto-Norman kings a different situation is perhaps apparent, a situation where, under the patronage of the Lordship of the Isles, the basic way of life can remain unchanged until the seventeenth century (Crawford, 1967; archaeological demonstration, Crawford, 1972). Perhaps here the re-occupation of duns sometimes made use of their original defensive structure, or modified it as at Dun Lagaidh. However, too much should not be read into the persistence of patterns of re-occupation of prehistoric sites into historic times. What it demonstrates is no more than that the same areas were favoured for settlement in medieval as in later prehistoric times, a fact less surprising than it might at first seem when it is remembered how much of Highland Scotland was quite unsuited to human settlement.

A notable feature of all the sites is their relatively small size. Where earlier Iron Age sites were re-occupied in the post-Roman period, there is evidence for a reduction in the area of occupation. Without extensive excavation it is impossible to calculate how much of any given fort was occupied in the post-Roman period, but it is not impossible that only the citadel or inner defensive work was occupied and that the outworks served as cattle kraals. Bradley and others have already stressed the possible origin of some hillforts of the southern British Iron Age in earlier Bronze Age stock enclosures (Bradley, 1971, 71-2), and it is becoming increasingly clear that the outer enclosures often associated with Iron Age forts represent cattle enclosures, wherein the chief could display his wealth, while some of the sprawling forts of Wessex and adjacent areas may have been primarily intended as stock enclosures (Cunliffe, 1974, 254). If stock raising was important in the pre-Roman Iron Age, it was more so in the post-Roman

Celtic world, though agriculture played a greater part than is suggested by documentary sources. Irish documentary sources show very clearly that wealth was estimated in cattle (Proudfoot, 1961, 119) and on some sites cattle bones occur in vast numbers; at Cahercommaun, Co. Clare, they amounted to 97% of all the bones on the site (Hencken, 1938, 75). Cahercommaun presents an interesting comparison with citadel enclosures in Scotland. Here the structural remains comprised a stone-walled fort rather like a large dun within a complex of outworks comprising two concentric walls linked with cross walls, which the excavator suggested were cattle enclosures (Hencken, 1938, 10) (Fig. 24). At Garryduff, Co. Cork, one of two adjacent ringforts was interpreted by the excavator as being used purely as a cattle compound (O'Kelly, 1962, 124). This use of outworks as cattle enclosures would make even more explicable the occurrence of citadels within already ruinous forts where there is little evidence for any refurbishing of the ramparts, as at Turin Hill or Dunearn. If the outworks were simply to contain cattle, substantial ramparts would not be required and any deficiency in existing ramparts could be made good by a fence. While this explains the construction of 'citadels' within existing defences of Iron Age origin, it does not explain the purely Dark Age constructions like Dunadd where there were clearly huts in the outer enclosures and where it would be difficult to drive cattle up the rock. Here one should probably think in terms of the chief occupying the citadel and his family or followers occupying the outer enclosures. In this sense Dark Age sites reflect clearly the social changes between the first and fifth centuries A.D., with a move away from the large tribal group with its tribal capital to the smaller clan under its leader. The Mote of Mark probably did not support a population of more than about 25 persons, and Dunadd would have been crowded with more than fifty living on its summit. Few duns could have comfortably accommodated more than a dozen. Very few of the putative Dark Age forts in Scotland occupy an area much more than 500 ft (150 m) across, exceptions being perhaps Dundurn, which is over 1000 ft (300 m) across, and Dalmahoy which is over 1200 ft (360 m), but in each of these cases this is the result of the straggling nature of the outer enclosures, both sites having citadels of small dimensions: 150 ft (45 m) across at Dalmahoy, 70 ft (21 m) across at Dundurn. This settlement pattern compares closely with that of raths in Ireland, the rath or ringfort representing the farmstead of a 60 acre (25 ha) farm (Proudfoot, 1961; Proudfoot, 1970). Although the density of putatively post-Roman sites in Scotland rules out the interpretation of the post-Roman Scottish forts simply as farmsteads of an extended family, it is certainly not necessary to envisage them as either the capitals of miniature kingdoms or as military centres.

ACKNOWLEDGEMENT

I am indebted to Miss Nancy Edwards for her help in preparing the illustrations for this monograph.

ABBREVIATIONS

Arch. J.	Archaeological Journal
Arch. Ael.	Archaeologia Aeliana
Arch. Camb.	Archaeologia Cambrensis
Arch. N.L.	Archaeological Newsletter
Current Arch.	Current Archaeology
D. & E.	Discovery and Excavation in Scotland
G.A.J.	Glasgow Archaeological Journal
Inv.E.Loth.	R.C.H.A.M. Inventory of East Lothian
Inv.Rox.	R.C.H.A.M. Inventory of Roxburghshire
Inv.Stirl.	R.C.H.A.M. Inventory of Stirlingshire
Inv.Wigt.	R.C.H.A.M. Inventory of Wigtownshire
J.R.S.A.I.	Journal of the Royal Society of Antiquaries of Ireland
Med.Arch.	Medieval Archaeology
P.P.S.	Proceedings of the Prehistoric Society
P.R.I.A.	Proceedings of the Royal Irish Academy
P.S.A.S.	Proceedings of the Society of Antiquaries of Scotland
Post-Med.Arch.	Post-Medieval Archaeology
S.A.F.	Scottish Archaeological Forum
S.H.R.	Scottish Historical Review
Trans.Bute N.H.S.	Transactions of the Buteshire Natural History Society
Trans.D. & G.N.H.A.S.	Transactions of the Dumfries & Galloway Natural History and Antiquarian Society
U.J.A.	Ulster Journal of Archaeology
L.M.C.	London Museum Medieval Catalogue

BIBLIOGRAPHY

ALCOCK, L.	1963	Dinas Powys, an Iron Age, Dark Age and Medieval Settlement in Glamorgan, Cardiff, (1963).
ALCOCK, L.	1965	'Wales in the Fifth to Seventh Centuries A.D.; Archaeological Evidence' in Foster, I. & Daniel, G. (Eds.), Prehistoric and Early Wales, London, (1965), 177-212.
ALCOCK, L.	1967	'Excavations at Degannwy Castle, Caernarvonshire', Arch.J. CXXIV (1967), 190-201.
ALCOCK, L.	1970	'Was There an Irish Sea Culture Province in the Dark Ages?' in Moore, D. (Ed.), The Irish Sea Province in Archaeology and History, (1970), 55-65.
ALCOCK, L.	1971	Arthur's Britain, London, (1971).
ALCOCK, L.	1972	By South Cadbury is that Camelot, London, (1972).
ANDERSON, J.	1878-9	'Notice of a Mortar and Lion Figures of Brass', P.S.A.S. New Ser. 1, (1878-9), 48-64.
ANDERSON, J.	1881	Scotland in Early Christian Times, Edinburgh, (1881).
ATKINSON, R.J.C.	1962	'Fishermen and Farmers', in Piggott, S. (Ed.), Prehistoric Peoples of Scotland, (1962), 1-38.
BALFOUR, J.A. (Ed.)	1910	The Book of Arran: Archaeology, (1910).
BARBOUR, J.	1906-7	'Notice of a Stone Fort near Kirkandrews, Kirkcudbrightshire', P.S.A.S. XLI (1906-7), 66-80.
BEVERIDGE, E.	1903	Coll and Tiree, Edinburgh, (1903).
BEVERIDGE, E.	1930-31	'Excavation of an earth-house at Foshigarry and a fort, Dun Tomaidh, North Uist', P.S.A.S. LV (1930-31), 299-356.
BOGLE, L.	1894-5	'Notes on some prehistoric structures in Glenelg and Kintail', P.S.A.S. XXIX (1894-5), 180-90.

BRADLEY, R.	1971	'Economic Change in the Growth of Early Hill-forts', in Jesson, M. & Hill, D. (Eds.), The Iron Age and its Hill-forts, Southampton, (1971), 71-84.
BURLEY, E.	1955-56	'A Survey of the Metalwork from Traprain Law', P.S.A.S. LXXXIX (1955-56), 118-226.
CALLANDER, J.G. & BEVERIDGE, E.	1931-2	'Earth-house at Garry Iochdrach and Bac Mhic Connain, in North Uist', P.S.A.S. LXVI (1931-2), 33-66.
CHILDE, V.G.	1940-41	'The defences of Kaimes Hill Fort, Midlothian', P.S.A.S. LXXV (1940-41), 43-54.
CHRISTISON, D.	1898	Early Fortifications in Scotland, Edinburgh (1898).
CHRISTISON, D.	1903-4	'The forts of Kilmartin, Kilmichael Glassary, and North Knapdale, Argyle', P.S.A.S. XXXVIII (1903-4), 205-51.
CHRISTISON, D.	1904-5	'Excavation of forts in the Poltalloch Estate, Argyll, in 1904-5', P.S.A.S. XXXIX (1904-5), 292-322.
CLARKE, D.	1971	'Small Finds in the Atlantic Province: Problems of Approach', S.A.F. 3, (1971), 22-54.
COLLINS, A.E.P.	1955	'Excavations at Lough Faughan Crannog, Co. Down', U.J.A. XXIX (1955), 45-82.
CRAW, J.H.	1929-30	'Excavations at Dunadd and other sites in the Poltalloch Estates, Argyll', P.S.A.S. LXIV (1929-30), 111-27.
CRAWFORD, I.A.	1964	A Preliminary Report of Excavations at Udal, North Uist , Edinburgh, (1964).
CRAWFORD, I.A.	1965	'Contribution to a History of Domestic Settlement in North Uist', Scottish Studies, IX (1965), 34-63.
CRAWFORD, I.A.	1967	'The Divide between Medieval and Post-medieval in Scotland', Post-Med.Arch. I, (1967), 84-9.

CRAWFORD, I.A.	1972	Excavations at Coileaghan an Udail (The Udal) N. Uist, - 9th Interim Report, (1972), Cambridge.
CRUDEN, S.H.	1965	'Excavations at Birsay, Orkney', in Small, A. (Ed.), Transactions of the Fourth Viking Congress, Aberdeen, (1965), 22-31.
CUNLIFFE, B.W.	1974	Iron Age Communities in Britain, London, (1974).
CURLE, A.O.	1913-14	'Report... on a Vitrified Fort at Rockcliffe, Dalbeattie, known as the Mote of Mark', P.S.A.S. XLVIII (1913-14), 125-68.
CURLE, A.O.	1914-15	'Account of Excavations on Traprain Law... in 1914', P.S.A.S. XLIX (1914-15), 139-202.
CURLE, A.O.	1938-39	'A Viking Settlement at Freswick, Caithness', P.S.A.S. LXXIII (1938-9), 71-110.
FAIRBAIRN, A.	1936-7	'Excavation of a Medieval site on Donald's Isle, Loch Doon', P.S.A.S. LXXI (1936-7), 323-333.
FAIRHURST, H.	1938-9	'A galleried dun at Kildonan Bay, Kintyre', P.S.A.S. LXXXIII (1938-9), 185-228.
FAIRHURST, H.	1954-56	'The stack fort on Ugadale Point, Kintyre', P.S.A.S. LXXXVIII (1954-56), 15-22.
FAIRHURST, H.	1961-2	'An Caisteal: an Iron Age fortification in Mull', P.S.A.S. XCV (1961-2), 199-207.
FAIRHURST, H.	1969	'A Mediaeval island-settlement in Loch Glashan, Argyll', G.A.J. I, (1969), 47-67.
FEACHEM, R.	1955	'Fortifications', in Wainwright, F.T. (Ed.), The Problem of the Picts, (1955).
FEACHEM, R.	1955-56	'The Fortifications on Traprain Law', P.S.A.S. LXXXIX (1955-56), 284-289.
FEACHEM, R.	1963	A Guide to Prehistoric Scotland, London (1966).

40

FEACHEM, R.	1966	'The hill-forts of Northern Britain', in Rivet, A.L.F. (Ed.), <u>The Iron Age in Northern Britain</u>, (1966), 59-88.
FOWLER, E.	1960	'The Origins and Development of the penannular brooch in Europe', <u>P.P.S.</u> XXVI (1960), 149-77.
FOWLER, E.	1963	'Celtic metalwork of the fifth and sixth centuries A.D.', <u>Arch.J.</u> CXX (1963), 98-160.
FOWLER, P.	1970	'Cadcong 1970', <u>Current Arch.</u> II (1970), 337-42.
FOWLER, P.	1971	'Hillforts A.D. 400-700', in Jesson, M. & Hill, D., <u>The Iron Age and its Hill-forts,</u> Southampton, (1971), 203-13.
GARDNER, W. & SAVORY, H.N.	1964	<u>Dinorben</u>, Cardiff, (1964).
GELLING, P.	1957-65	'Recent Excavations of Norse Houses in the Isle of Man', <u>J.Manx Mus.</u> VI (1957-65), 54-6.
GELLING, P.	1962-3	'Medieval shielings in the Isle of Man', <u>Med.Arch.</u> VI-VII, (1962-3), 156-72.
GELLING, P.	1969	'A metalworking site at Kiondroghad, Kirk Andreas, Isle of Man', <u>Med.Arch.</u> XIII (1969), 67-83.
GRAHAM CAMPBELL, J.	1972	'A group of ninth century Irish Brooches', <u>J.R.S.A.I.</u> CII (1972), 113-28.
GRIEG, C.	1972	'Cullykhan', <u>Current Arch.</u> III, (1972), 227-31.
HAMILTON, J.R.C.	1956	<u>Excavations at Jarlshof, Shetland,</u> Edinburgh, (1956).
HENCKEN, H.O'N.	1938	<u>Cahercommaun, a Stone Fort in Co. Clare,</u> (1938).
HENCKEN, H.O'N.	1950	'Lagore, a royal residence of the 7th to 10th centuries A.D.', <u>P.R.I.A.</u> LIII (1950), 1-247.
HENSHALL, A.S.	1955-6	'The long cist cemetery at Parkburn, Midlothian', <u>P.S.A.S.</u> LXXXIX (1955-56), 252-83.
HOGG, A.H.A.	1960	'Garn Boduan and Tr'er Ceiri', <u>Arch.J.</u> CXVII (1960), 1-39.

Henderson 1967 ? (P 28)

41

HOPE-TAYLOR, B.	1966	'Doon Hill', Med.Arch. X (1966), 176-7.
JOBEY, G.	1959	'Excavation at the native site of Huckhoe, Northumberland', Arch.Ael. 4th ser. XXXVII (1959), 217-78.
KILBRIDE-JONES, H.	1935-6	'Scots Zoomorphic penannular brooches', P.S.A.S. LXX (1935-6), 124-38.
KILBRIDE-JONES, H.	1937	'The Evolution of penannular brooches with zoomorphic terminals in Great Britain and Ireland', P.R.I.A. XLIII,C, (1936-7), 379-455.
LAING, L.	1969a	'Timber Halls in Dark Age Britain - Some Problems', Trans.D.&G.N.H.A.S. XLVI (1969), 110-127.
LAING, L.	1969b	'Scottish medieval settlement archaeology S.A.F. 1, (1969), 69-79.
LAING, L.	1973	'The Mote of Mark', Current Arch. IV (1973), 121-25.
LAING, L.	1974a	Orkney and Shetland: an Archaeological Guide, Newton Abbot, (1974).
LAING, L.	1974b	'Cooking pots and the origins of the Scottish medieval pottery industry', Arch.J. CXXX (1974), 183-216.
LAING, L.	1975	The Archaeology of Late Celtic Britain and Ireland, c.400-1200 A.D., London (1975).
LETHBRIDGE, T.	1952	'Excavations at Kilphedir, S.Uist, and the problems of brochs and wheelhouses', P.P.S. XVIII (1952), 176-193.
MACKENZIE, W.M.	1904-5	'Structures of Archaic type in the Island of Lewis...', P.S.A.S. XXXVIII (1904-5), 173-204.
MACKIE, E.	1965	'The origin and development of the broch and wheelhouse building vultures of the Scottish Iron Age', P.P.S. XXXI (1965), 132-3.
MACKIE, E.	1968	Excavations on Loch Broom, Ross & Cromarty, second interim report, 1968, Glasgow, (1968).

MACKIE, E.	1969	'Radiocarbon dates and the Scottish Iron Age', Ant. XLIII (1969), 15-26.
MACKIE, E.	1970	'The Scottish Iron Age: a Review', S.H.R. XLIX (1970), 2-32.
MARSHALL, D.	1965	Report on the Excavations at Little Dunagoil, (Trans. Bute N.H.S. XVI, 1965).
MAXWELL, G.	1969	'Duns and Forts - a note on some Iron Age monuments of the Atlantic Province', S.A.F. 1 (1969), 41-52.
NEWALL, F.	1960	Excavations at Walls Hill, Renfrewshire, Paisley, (1960).
NEWALL, F.	1965	Excavations at Knapps, Renfrewshire, Paisley, (1965).
NORMAN, E. & ST JOSEPH, J.K.	1969	The Early Development of Irish Society, Cambridge, (1969).
O'KELLY, M.J.	1962	'Two Ring-forts at Garryduff, Co.Cork', P.R.I.A. LXIII, (1962), 17-125.
PIGGOTT, C.M.	1947-8	'The Excavations at Hownam Rings, Roxburghshire, 1948', P.S.A.S. LXXXII (1947-8), 193-224.
PIGGOTT, C.M.	1949-50	'The Excavations at Bonchester Hill, 1950', P.S.A.S. LXXXIV (1949-50), 113-37.
PIGGOTT, C.M.	1952-3	'Milton Loch Crannog I: a native house of the second century A.D. in Kirkcudbrightshire', P.S.A.S. LXXXVII (1952-3), 134-52.
PIGGOTT, S.	1957-8	'Excavations at Braidwood Fort, Midlothian', P.S.A.S. XLI (1957-8), 61-77.
PROUDFOOT, V.B.	1956	'Excavations at Cathedral Hill, Downpatrick', U.J.A. XIX (1956), 57-72.
PROUDFOOT, V.B.	1961	'The economy of the Irish rath', Med. Arch. V (1961), 94-122.
PROUDFOOT, V.B.	1970	'Irish raths and cashels: some notes on origins, chronology and survivals', U.J.A. XXXIII (1970), 37-48.
RADFORD, C.A.R.	1962	'From Prehistory to History', in Piggott, S. (Ed.), The Prehistoric Peoples of Scotland, London, (1962), 125-54.

RAFTERY, B.	1972	'Irish Hill-forts', in Thomas, C. (Ed.) The Iron Age in the Irish Sea Province, London, (1972), 37-58.
RAHTZ, P. & FOWLER, P.	1972	'Somerset A.D. 400-700', in Fowler, P. (Ed.), Archaeology and the Landscape, London, (1972), 187-221.
RITCHIE, G.	1968-9	'Two New Pictish Symbol Stones from Orkney', P.S.A.S. CI (1968-9), 130-33.
RITCHIE, J.	1941-2	'The Lake-dwelling or Crannog in Eadarloch, Loch Trieg: its traditions and construction', P.S.A.S. LXXVI (1941-2), 8-78.
ROUSSELL, A.	1934	Norse Building Customs in the Scottish Isles, (1934).
SAVORY, H.	1960	'Excavations at Dinas Emrys, Beddgelert Caernarvonshire', Arch.Camb. CIX (1960), 13-77.
SCOTT, J.	1961	'Loch Glashan Crannog', Med.Arch. V (1961), 310.
SCOTT, L.	1948	'Gallo-British colonies: the aisled round-house culture in the north', P.P.S. XIV (1948), 46-125.
SELKIRK, A.	1969	'Dun Lagaidh', Current Arch. II (1969), 8-13.
SHETELIG, H.	1954	Viking Antiquities of Great Britain and Ireland, VI (1954), Oslo.
SIMPSON, D.	1969	'Excavations at Kaimes Hillfort, Midlothian', G.A.J. 1, (1969), 7-28.
SMALL, A.	1964-6	'Excavations at Underhoull, Shetland', P.S.A.S. XCVIII (1964-66), 225-248.
SMALL, A.	1969	'Burghead', S.A.F. 1, (1969), 61-8.
SMALL, A.	1972	Craig Phadrig, Dundee, (1972).
SMITH, J.	1918-19	'Excavation of the Forts of Castlehill, ... and Coalhill, Ayrshire', P.S.A.S. LIII (1918-19).
STEER, K. & KEENEY, G.	1946-7	'Excavations in two Homesteads at Crock Cleugh, Roxburghshire', P.S.A.S. LXXXI (1946-7), 138-
STEVENSON, R.B.K.	1942-3	'Medieval Dwelling sites and a primitive village in the parish of Manor, Peeblesshire', P.S.A.S. LXXV (1942-3), 92-115.

STEVENSON, R.B.K. 1948-9 'The nuclear fort of Dalmahoy and other Dark Age capitals', P.S.A.S. LXXXIII (1948-9), 186-97.

STEVENSON, R.B.K. 1955 'Pins and the Chronology of Brochs', P.P.S. XXI (1955), 282-94.

THOMAS, A.C. 1959 'Imported Pottery in Dark Age Western Britain', Med.Arch. III (1959), 89-111.

THOMAS, A.C. 1961 'Excavations at Trusty's Hill, Anwoth, 1960', Trans. D. & G.N.H.A.S. XXVIII (1961), 58-70.

THOMAS, A.C. 1961b 'The Animal Art of the Scottish Iron Age', Arch.J. CXVIII (1961), 14-64.

THOMAS, A.C. 1966 'Ardwall Isle: The Excavation of an Early Christian site of Irish Type, 1964-5', Trans. D. & G.N.H.A.S. XLIII (1966), 84-116.

THOMAS, A.C. 1968 'The Evidence from North Britain', in Barley, M. & Hanson, R. (Eds.), Christianity in Britain, 300-700, Leicester, (1968), 93-122.

THOMAS, A.C. 1971 The Early Christian Archaeology of North Britain, Oxford, (1971).

TRUCKELL, A.E. & WILLIAMS, J. 1967 'Medieval Pottery in Dumfriesshire and Galloway', Trans. D. & G.N.H.A.S. XLIV (1967), 133-74.

WAINWRIGHT, F.T. 1963 The Souterrains of Southern Pictland, London, (1963).

WAINWRIGHT, G. 1967 Coygan Camp, Glamorgan, Cardiff, (1967).

WATSON, W.J. 1912-13 'The circular forts of North Perthshire', P.S.A.S. XLVII (1912-13), 30-60.

WILLIAMS, J. 1971a 'Tynron Doon, Dumfriesshire: a History of the Site with notes on the finds, 1924-67', Trans. D. & G.N.H.A.S. XLVIII (1971), 106-20.

WILLIAMS, J. 1971b 'A crannog at Loch Arthur, New Abbey', Trans. D. & G.N.H.A.S. XLVIII (1971), 121-4.

YOUNG, A. 1952-3 'An aisled farmhouse at Allasdale, Isle of Barra', P.S.A.S. LXXXVII (1952-3), 80-105.

YOUNG, A.	1955-56	'Excavations at Dun Cuier, Isle of Barra', <u>P.S.A.S.</u> LXXXIX (1955-56), 290-328.
YOUNG, A.	1961-2	'Brochs and Duns', <u>P.S.A.S.</u> XCV (1961-2), 171-98.
YOUNG, A.	1966	'The Sequence of Hebridean Pottery', in Rivet, A.L.F. (Ed.), <u>The Iron Age in Northern Britain</u>, (1966), 45-58.
YOUNG, A. & RICHARDSON, K.	1959-60	'A Cheardach Mhor, Dirmore, S.Uist', <u>P.S.A.S.</u> XCIII (1959-60), 135-73.

www.ingramcontent.com/pod-product-compliance
Lightning Source LLC
Chambersburg PA
CBHW051309270326
41929CB00029B/3473